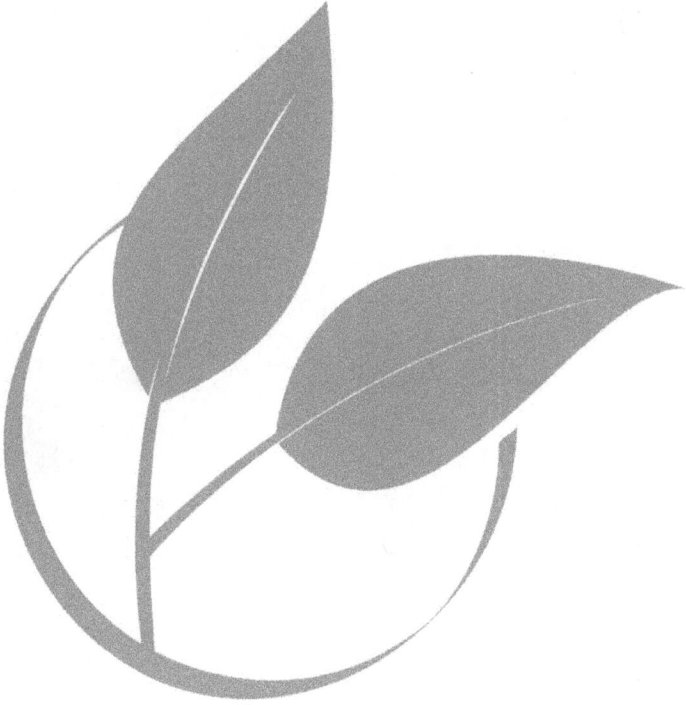

PHILIPPIANS: GROWING IN OUR LOVE FOR JESUS AND FOR ONE ANOTHER

BY TOBY LOGSDON

Philippians: Growing in Our Love For Jesus and For One Another

Copyright © 2014 by Toby Logsdon. All rights reserved.

Designed by Toby Logsdon

Published in association with BibleStudyPodcasts.Org

First edition

ISBN 978-0-6922-2080-1

Contents

Chapter 1: Introduction

Philippians 1:1-6

The book of Philippians is known as the most delightful letter that Paul wrote. Even though this letter was composed while Paul was imprisoned, there is no other letter that was written by Paul which contains as much praise and rejoicing. This is, after all, the book where Paul writes, "Rejoice in the Lord, always! Again, I will say rejoice!" That's ironic, isn't it? Because we tend to operate in the opposite direction: when life is good and things are going our way, rejoicing comes naturally. And when things are tough, all of a sudden we become people who are serious about prayer. But rejoicing in the midst of hardship? That's something that doesn't come naturally or easily.

Paul was a church-planter. It was his calling, and it was his gifting. And Paul always gravitated toward major cities of his day. If he was planting churches today, I have no doubt that he would be looking at cities just like the one I live in—Seattle—as the ideal type of place to bring the gospel. That's why he was so eager to pay a visit to the city of Rome, which would have been the biggest city he had ever seen in his day and age. But Philippi was also a fairly large metropolitan city. In fact, it was modeled after Rome's likeness, with giant Roman arches, bathhouses, forums, and temples that looked just like what you would see in the city of Rome.

The city had enormous temples and altars which had been dedicated to the worship of the emperor and his family members. The emperor was the primary object of worship in the city, and historians tell us that failure to participate in this imperial cult was viewed by its faithful adherents as a type of subversive activity. It was a city of zealous, deeply-committed idolaters who were passionate about their idol-worship. Sounds a lot like modern America.

As we're going to see, Paul had some very fond memories of his friends in the city of Philippi. But while he had some strong affections for these friends, and desired to write to them in order to affirm them in their ministry, he also wrote to respond to some of the issues that they were facing. There's no such thing as a ministry that never faces any issues of some type or another! As we study this letter, we'll see that he's going to address several important issues, such as the way that things like pride and gossip were dividing fellow believers, the skepticism and hostility from the world that surrounded the Philippian church, and the so-called spirituality of religious leaders who had come up with a bogus formula—a perversion of the gospel—as a means of attracting converts and boasting in their own success. Again, you would think that I was describing the church in twenty-first century America, wouldn't you?

God wants us to grow in two very important ways: in our love for Christ, and in our selfless love for our fellow brothers and sisters who are in Christ. These are the two primary themes of the book of Philippians. If a person is stagnant/lifeless/dead in either of these two qualities, they should fear for their salvation. This is serious stuff that you have to be insane to take lightly. That's why the Apostle John said, "If anyone says, 'I love God,' and hates his brother, he is a liar; for he who does not love his brother whom he has seen cannot love God whom he has not seen" (1st John 4:20). We should consider ourselves warned.

The letter to the Philippians is about growing, both in our love for Jesus and in our love for one another. Closely related to that theme is the theme of growing in our likeness to Christ. I have a feeling that if either Paul or John could look at the state of the church in America, they would be shocked. I've seen people leave a church because they don't like the music, or because the guy down the street keeps his sermons under 35 minutes, or this church on the other side of town has a new program that they're doing. Do you realize how crazy all of this looks when we compare it to the church in the first century? God designed the church to be an unstoppable force—so unstoppable that Jesus said that we would be beating down the gates of hell, and the gates of hell wouldn't be able to stand against His kingdom!

The first century church was constantly looking out for one another, and they were committed to sticking together despite differences of opinion on minor issues. They were like a family that was, sure, less than perfect at times, but who loved and stood by each other. And I suspect that if someone like Paul or John could look at our churches these days, they'd be absolutely heart-broken, because we have churches splitting over things like who gets to decide what color the carpet is going to be, how strong the coffee in the coffee pot should be, or how short should the grass lawn be mowed down to. I am not kidding; I've either known the pastors or I've heard about churches that have gone through these very exact things.

This epistle is written to a church that very easily could have gone down that way, but they didn't. Why do I say that they could have? Consider the story of how the church in Philippi got started:

"So, setting sail from Troas, we made a direct voyage to Samothrace, and the following day to Neapolis, and from there to Philippi, which is a leading city of the district of Macedonia and a Roman colony. We remained in this city some days. And on the Sabbath day we went outside the gate to the riverside, where we supposed there was a place of prayer, and we sat down and spoke to the women who had come together. One who heard us was a woman named Lydia, from the city of Thyatira, a seller of purple goods, who was a worshiper of God. The Lord opened her heart to pay attention to what was said by Paul. And after she was baptized, and her household as well, she urged us, saying, 'If you have judged me to be faithful to the Lord, come to my house and stay.' And she prevailed upon us." (Acts 16:11-15)

Paul's custom, when he came into a city, was always to go straight to the local synagogue to show the Jews from the Old Testament Scriptures that Jesus, the Messiah had come just as God had promised, and that He had died and risen again. But there were no synagogues in Philippi. Instead, all they could find was a place that was designated as a place of prayer. If that alone wasn't an indication that this was a place that had a desperate need for the Gospel, I don't know what is!

Basically, what Paul came across is the modern-day equivalent to a Sunday morning women's Bible study. But there appears to be a subtle indication that most of the women here were part of the local cult that worshiped the emperor and his family. After all, out of all of the women that Paul and his team encountered, only one was said to worship the one true God: a woman named Lydia, who was from the city of Thyatira. The people of Thyatira were known for selling what Luke calls "purple goods." Lydia, in other words, sells upscale clothing. It's possible that she was something of a fashion queen. She seems to have made a good living for herself and for her household. And as soon as Paul started showing her what the Old Testament said about the Messiah and how Jesus fit the profile, the Lord opened her heart to hear, and she was converted on the spot.

Her response was to bring her family over to meet Paul and hear him speak. Paul and his team of missionaries shared the gospel with everyone in her family, and boom—the Lord opens their hearts and they were all converted as well, and they all got baptized, apparently on the spot.

So far so good, right? Not so fast. You know that the enemy of God hates it when even one fewer person will be joining him in hell, and so where there is success, the enemy will be sure to cause opposition to rise up. That's what we see as we continue to study the founding of the church in Philippi.

"As we were going to the place of prayer, we were met by a slave girl who had a spirit of divination and brought her owners much gain by fortune-telling. She followed Paul and us, crying out, 'These men are servants of the Most High God, who proclaim to you the way of salvation.' And this she kept doing for many days." (Acts 16:16-18a)

Now, on the surface, we might say, "What's the big deal? Why is this a problem?" After all, she was proclaiming the truth, wasn't she? She wasn't lying or anything. But she was distracting. She was affirming that these men had come with the message that leads to salvation in such a way that the people would hear her affirmation, but they wouldn't hear the message of the gospel, because she was drawing all of the attention to herself. Not only that, but she was screaming it out like a crazy woman. And let's think about this: who was going to believe what a crazy woman is saying? So while she was affirming the message that Paul and his team of missionaries were proclaiming, she was stealing their credibility by acting crazy. She was not crazy though—she was possessed by demonic spirits. And so finally, after several surely exhausting days of this, Paul had enough.

"Paul, having become greatly annoyed, turned and said to the spirit, 'I command you in the name of Jesus Christ to come out of her.' And it came out that very hour." (Acts 16:18b)

I want us to see the contrast between Lydia and this girl. Lydia owned her own business; this girl was a slave whose master turned a profit on her fortune-telling. Lydia worshiped God; this girl mocked God and served demons. Lydia listened to Paul; this girl was constantly interrupting Paul. And when Paul reached a breaking point, commanding the demonic spirits to leave her, she found freedom in the very name she had been going around mocking—the mighty name of Jesus.

And if you thought that this was interesting, you haven't seen anything yet.

"But when her owners saw that their hope of gain was gone, they seized Paul and Silas and dragged them into the marketplace before the rulers. And when they had brought them to the magistrates, they said, 'These men are Jews, and they are disturbing our city. They advocate customs that are not lawful for us as Romans to accept or practice.'" (Acts 16:19-21)

What customs would those be? Worshiping God. In the verses that follow, we learn that the leaders and the crowd that had gathered decided to beat Paul and his team of missionaries with rods. But wait, there's more! They also got thrown into prison, where the jailer put Paul and Silas in stocks.

We have such a comfortable idea of what it means to be put in stocks. If you're like most people, you probably imagine that it was just like the stocks that you could have expected to find in the Renaissance era, in which the would have their head, hands, and feet stuck facing the same way in this contraption. But that's not what the stocks of the first century were like. In the first century, they would force a prisoner to twist and turn their bodies in very unnatural ways, causing the muscles in their bodies to go into sudden, painful cramps, and they'd just leave them like that for days. So what kind of a man do you think you'd have to be if you were a jailer? You'd be thick-skinned, hard-hearted, and just plain old mean. You wouldn't be the type of guy I'd want to run into in a dark alley. And the truth about these kinds of guys was that they didn't mind the cruelty. They couldn't do their job without a seared conscience. Maybe there was even a part of them that enjoyed hearing the screams of agony.

But as much joy as a man like this might have gotten from his job, he didn't have more joy than Paul or Silas that night. Despite their bodies being stuck in contorted positions, we read this:

"About midnight Paul and Silas were praying and singing hymns to God, and the prisoners were listening to them, and suddenly there was a great earthquake, so that the foundations of the prison were shaken. And immediately all the doors were opened, and everyone's bonds were unfastened. When the jailer woke and saw that the prison doors were open, he drew his sword and was about to kill himself, supposing that the prisoners had escaped." (Acts 16:25-27)

Do not miss Paul's attitude, because it reaps dividends in life's hardest situations. This is a guy who doesn't care if you don't like what he has to say. "Am I trying to please man? If I were still trying to please man, I would not be a servant of Christ." You want to just make his life as difficult as possible? He says, "To live is Christ." You want to kill him? He says, "To die is gain." You can't win against a faith like Paul's, because he was unswervingly committed to living for no purpose beyond the glory of God. If you had been this jailer, you would probably have felt just a little irritated that Paul and Silas had been praying and singing hymns of praise all night while hurting in ways that most of us have never experienced.

But then an earthquake came, and it was strong enough that all of the stocks were rattled loose, and all of these prisoners that the jail keeper was responsible for were suddenly free. And so the jailer was about to take his own life, because in Paul's day, the jailer would pay for the life of an escaped prisoner with his own life.

But Paul was prepared to throw a life line to the jailer by sharing the only source of true hope with him. Rather than seeing this as an opportunity to flee, Paul saw it as an opportunity to share the Gospel with the jailer. And so rather than fleeing, Paul assured the jailer that even though they could go free, they wouldn't.

"And the jailer called for lights and rushed in, and trembling with fear he fell down before Paul and Silas. Then he brought them out and said, 'Sirs, what must I do to be saved?' And they said, 'Believe in the Lord Jesus, and you will be saved, you and your household.' And they spoke the word of the Lord to him and to all who were in his house. And he took them the same hour of the night and washed their wounds; and he was baptized at once, he and all his family. Then he brought them up into his house and set food before them. And he rejoiced along with his entire household that he had believed in God." (Acts 16:29-34)

At this point, the team of Philippian church-planters is in place: a businesswoman, a man who was probably so tough that he ate nails for breakfast, and possibly even this slave girl who had once been possessed by demons. Honestly, you can't look at this and believe that anyone is outside of the reach of the Lord. If these three can be changed into new creations, God can change ANYONE into a new creation!

What we see is that the church in Philippi flies right in the face of human nature, which is to surround ourselves with people who are just like us. Why? Because the flesh nature dictates that we love ourselves so much that we can't stand being surrounded by people who are different from us or who believe even slightly differently than we do—even on minor issues. This is what sociologists call "the principle of homogeneity." It means that we only like to be with people who are just like us. But the gospel calls us to look beyond surface demographics, which is why Paul encouraged the Corinthians not to regard people according to the flesh—to stop judging by human standards, but to look deeper than the surface with people.

This is something that characterized the church in Philippi from the very start. As different as these people are from one another, do you think this church might have struggled with personality conflicts? Absolutely. But this is the only church that Paul wrote to, saying, "How I long for you all with the affection of Christ Jesus" (1:8). Nobody else—no other church who got a letter from the Apostle Paul—got words like that from him. But he loved this church, personality conflicts and all, because they made it work. And the only reason it worked? They were committed to growing in their love for Christ and their love for one another. This is a message that the American church as a whole needs badly right now, if we ever hope to show the world that the church really is the unstoppable force that Jesus promised it would be!

These are the people of whom Paul is so fond. And thus he writes them a letter, which will ultimately be an encouragement for them to grow. He starts in typical fashion, writing:

"Paul and Timothy, servants of Christ Jesus, to all the saints in Christ Jesus who are at Philippi, with the overseers and deacons: Grace to you and peace from God our Father and the Lord Jesus Christ." (Philippians 1:1-2)

One of the things I always encourage people to look for when they're reading the Bible is repetition, because it means that the author wants to draw your attention to whatever it is that he's repeating. In just the first two verses, look at the repetition: "Christ Jesus," "Christ Jesus," and "the Lord Jesus Christ." I'm not even convinced that Paul did this intentionally (although the Holy Spirit, who inspired Paul to write this, surely did). I just think that the Lord Jesus was so central to Paul's life and his thinking and his very existence that this type of thing happened naturally for him. But the theme of Jesus Christ permeates everything that Paul has to say.

He identifies himself as a slave (or servant) of Christ Jesus, and he identifies his audience first and foremost as saints who are, by definition, in Christ Jesus. "In Philippi" is their secondary means of identification. Paul is giving us a great lesson in where to find our identity here, simply with the implications of what he's saying.

It's so easy for us to get caught up in categories that we lose sight of our primary identification, which is in Christ Jesus. And so we get people who define themselves by their race or their gender or their nationality or even the region of the nation they live in. Or how about this: people define themselves first and foremost by their sexuality. I think that, for me, that's one of the most disturbing things about many homosexuals. They find their identity, first and foremost, in their sexuality. Now, don't get me wrong— that's just as wrong as finding your identity first and foremost in your career, in your possessions, in your political party, or in anything other than Jesus Christ. So really, anyone who hasn't given Jesus their first priority in their life, and therefore doesn't find their identity primarily in Him, needs to repent of and turn from whatever they've placed before Him. And this is something that all of us struggle with.

So he's writing to the saints who are with the overseers and deacons. An overseer is a pastor, and a deacon wasn't an official position or anything like that with the early church. It was just someone who participated in the ministry of the local church in some capacity. So if we were to apply this definition to our church, we've got plenty of deacons as well: we have board members, we have people who help out with kid's church and nursery, we have someone who prints our bulletins, we have people who put the announcement videos together every week, we have someone who organizes ladies craft night, we have people who are in charge of the sound and the slides for the power-point. We have people who decorate the church. We have people who clean the church. These are all people who make ministry happen here. By definition, if we were speaking Greek, they would be called "deacons."

But this is the only instance in the entire book of Philippians that the pastors and workers in the church receive special recognition. From here on out, they're not even mentioned—at least not so specifically by title. But there's a good reason that Paul addresses them by title here: because those are the people who were the potential cause and/or solution to the problem of disunity being stirred up in the church.

Paul says, "Grace to you and peace from God our Father and the Lord Jesus Christ." This is a typical opening line for Paul. We sign our letters, "from" so and so, or "sincerely" so and so. If you're really super-spiritual, you sign your letters, "Blessings" so and so (yes, I'm being facetious). But Paul identifies himself and wishes God's grace and peace to them, almost as an opening benediction, similar to how he opens all of his epistles.

Now we move to the body of the letter:

"I thank my God in all my remembrance of you, always in every prayer of mine for you all making my prayer with joy, because of your partnership in the gospel from the first day until now." (Philippians 1:3-5)

The thing that I love about this is that he's already moved into teaching mode. As I mentioned earlier, this letter will focus on growing in our love for Christ and for each other. Loving Jesus is easy—there are plenty of people who say that they love Jesus . . . or at least they love the person that they imagine Him to be. Whether or not their understanding of Jesus is Biblically-valid is another issue. But loving Jesus is easy. But the fact is that a lot of Christians do more *groaning* about their brothers and sisters in Christ than they do *growing* in their love for them.

But Paul is teaching by example here. He's teaching that the Christian life is not to be done in isolation. If you're by yourself, you're not serving anyone but yourself. If you're by yourself, you can't be praying for or meeting the needs of your brothers and sisters in Christ. If you're by yourself, you're not accountable to anyone but yourself. There is no such thing as a healthy, growing, lone-ranger Christian. It's an oxymoron, just like when someone says that they're "terribly good" at something. Which is it? It can't be both! Likewise, you can't be a healthy lone-ranger if you're a Christian.

Jesus said, "A new commandment I give to you, that you love one another: just as I have loved you, you also are to love one another" (John 13:34). In fact, Jesus says that three times between John 13 and John 15. Remember what I said about repetition? Do you think that maybe Jesus wanted us to catch on to how important it is that we love one another? That's why John begs us, writing, "Beloved, if God so loved us, we also ought to love one another" (1st John 4:11). One of the main points that John makes in the book of 1st John is that loving one another is an unmistakable sign that a person has been born again! If you're not in fellowship with a local body of Christians, you're not loving them. And if you're not loving them, something is very, very wrong.

Think of how fire works, to illustrate how this all works. Fire needs at least two things: heat and oxygen. Do you think that you can make fire without both of those elements? Give it your best shot—it's not going to happen. Likewise, you will not have a healthy, vibrant Christian who is not both in fellowship with Christ and in fellowship with Christ's people.

And so Paul is a living example of what it means to be partnering with fellow believers. Even though he's not present with them, he's praying regularly for them. Every now and then I get a letter from someone saying that they love listening to BibleStudyPodcasts, but that they can't afford to support the ministry financially. And my response is typically something like this: "Your prayers are more powerful than your money. Please pray for me and pray for the ministry that God has entrusted to me!"

Paul recognizes that he can serve other believers through prayer, and he recognizes that he has a real need for other believers—even the ones who drove him crazy. Even the ones he didn't agree about absolutely everything on. Even the ones who had almost nothing in common with him— the fact that they were in Christ was sufficient common ground. Paul was thankful for all of them.

Finally, Paul writes:

"And I am sure of this, that he who began a good work in you will bring it to completion at the day of Jesus Christ." *(Philippians 1:6)*

This is the great hope of the Gospel: that God began a good work in us, and that God will complete what He has begun. There was a time when we were enemies of God, but through faith and repentance, He imputed our sins to Jesus and in exchange, transferred Jesus' righteousness to us. And so suddenly, we became citizens of another kingdom. Once we were citizens in the kingdom of darkness, and we desired only darkness. But we believed in Jesus and we repented—that is, we took full responsibility for and ownership of our sin, we opened our hearts up before God, allowing ourselves to stand transparent before Him, and we confessed and turned away from our sinfulness—and God transferred us into the Kingdom of Light. And this was just the beginning of what will be a life-long journey for all of us.

In the context of this letter, it's important for Paul to add this, because of the disharmony that was brewing in the church. The church is imperfect, and that's how every church in this life is always going to be; but it won't be imperfect forever. There will come a day when we stand before Jesus and He completes His work in us, fully perfecting us. Yes, Jesus said, "Be perfect, as your Father in heaven is perfect," but the context of that quote was when Jesus was trying to show the people who were listening to the Sermon on the Mount that even the best people among us fell short of God's standards. He was showing them their need for Him! Jesus prefaced this statement by saying, "For I tell you, unless your righteousness exceeds that of the scribes and Pharisees, you will never enter the kingdom of heaven" (Matthew 5:20).

Jesus wasn't instructing us to be perfect on our own; He was challenging the people who thought that they were good enough to get to heaven on their own!

The more mature a believer comes, the more they realize how far they are from perfect. That's why Paul goes on a rant in Romans 7 about his struggle with sin, and that's why John says that if anyone says that they're without sin, the truth is not in them. When we talk about Paul and John, we're talking about guys who personally saw Jesus, and even into their old age, when they looked at themselves, they realized that they were greatly imperfect in comparison with the sinless Savior.

God will complete what He has begun. But not in this life. Paul says that God's work in us will be completed on the day of Jesus Christ. John says, "Beloved, we are God's children now, and what we will be has not yet appeared; but we know that when he appears we shall be like him, because we shall see him as he is" (1st John 3:2). When we stand before Him and see Him one day, we'll instantly become like Him: sinless. And not a moment sooner. The great assurance here is that nothing will stand in the way of God's work in us being completed.

Until then, "We see in a mirror dimly, but then face to face. Now I know in part; then I shall know fully, even as I have been fully known" (1st Corinthians 13:12). God has begun a good work in us. Though we stumble and fall, He will complete it. Notice that it's the Lord who will complete it—not us. Until that day, let us continue to grow in our love for Him and for each other, knowing that problems and disagreements will sometimes rise up among us, but that love covers a multitude of sins.

~~~

Chapter 2: The Outward-Focused Life

Philippians 1:3-11

Can you imagine what it would have been like to receive a letter from Paul? I mean, think about this for a second. What if Paul wrote a letter specifically addressed to you and your church? How excited would you be? We're talking about the most influential Christian in history, by far (and no, Jesus was not a Christian . . . He's the Christ, the one that Christians follow and belong to). So what would it be like to receive a letter from him?

See, it was a big deal for the first century church—whichever church you want to talk about—to receive a letter from Paul. Why else do you think they'd preserve those letters? I mean, that's how they survived through the ages; the churches he wrote to cherished them! When Peter was writing his letters, he even went so far as to affirm that anything that Paul writes is Scripture (2nd Peter 3:15-16). And keep in mind that that was long before the church had an entire, canonized New Testament.

As we continue our study of the book of Philippians today, I want us to really think about the implications of what Paul is saying and how the Philippians would have felt about what Paul was saying. I am convinced that Paul knew that this was a pretty humble group of people. He was aware of the problems that they were facing, but he wasn't too concerned, really—not to the extent, at least, that he had been with the Galatians. But what we saw last week is that Paul was totally overflowing with joy and love toward the Philippians. I want us to start by reviewing what he said:

"I thank my God in all my remembrance of you, always in every prayer of mine for you all making my prayer with joy, because of your partnership in the gospel from the first day until now." (Philippians 1:3-5)

Here we see that Paul prayed for the church in Philippi. How often? Always. How did he pray? With joy, because of the partnership that Paul had with them from the very beginning of the church until the day that Paul wrote this, and no doubt extending forward into the future.

Could anyone possibly read this and miss the fact that Paul absolutely loved these people? This is the greatest sign that someone is a Christian: they love other Christians. Now, these aren't exactly perfect people that he's writing to. Not yet anyway, right? They had their flaws, their shortcomings, and their weaknesses . . . just like everyone else: just like you and I have flaws and weaknesses and just like every other Christian in the world has flaws and weaknesses. But when Paul thought of other believers, he saw a miracle in them. He saw people who were God's workmanship, people who were new creations in Christ Jesus. And so he loved them.

Have you ever thought about the fact that when you're talking about a believer in the Lord Jesus, you're talking to someone whose story is equally amazing as that of Lazarus, who was raised from literal, physical death? Because you and I HAVE been raised from death: spiritual death. And that is no less amazing than being raised from physical death. In fact, maybe it's even more amazing. God replaced our hearts of stone with hearts of living flesh. How long do you think you could physically live if you had a heart of stone? You couldn't live at all. And spiritually, a person has no life if they have not been made a new creation by God.

There are certain groups within Christianity that are constantly looking for various signs and wonders, and what you see is that when something does happen, it's almost always fraudulent. I'm heartbroken about this kind of thing, and I'm also disgusted by it. I hate hearing stories of people who go to church and are told that if their faith is strong enough, God is guaranteed to heal a life-long ailment that they have. And I think that the reason we have people who want to see these incredible signs and wonders is because some of us have lost the sense of wonder that we should have about the act of God giving spiritual life to someone who was once spiritually dead.

I recently watched the pilot episode of a TV show about zombies called "The Walking Dead." I couldn't exactly tell by the first episode where they plan on going with the show, and I'm not necessarily recommending it, because it's pretty gory (but hey, we're talking about a show about zombies), but there's this climactic scene toward the end of the episode in which the hero—a sheriff's deputy who hasn't been turned into a zombie (at least not yet)—rides into the city of Atlanta, thinking that the Center for Disease Control is located there, and so Atlanta must be a pretty safe place. But as he comes into the city, the streets look completely deserted. The city looks abandoned . . . that is, until he turns a corner, and suddenly there are thousands of zombies—the walking dead—who quickly surround him as he finds an abandoned army tank to take shelter in. And as the episode ends, the camera starts zooming up to the sky, revealing that there are thousands and thousands of walking dead closing in on him.

As I watched this, I thought to myself, "If the hearts of the unregenerate could be displayed externally, this is what the world would really look like." The unregenerate heart is overflowing with death, because death is the penalty of sin, and all have sinned.

Let's pretend that you could see people in that way. Can you imagine how amazing it would be to see someone changed from being one of the walking dead to one who is living? How amazing would it be to see someone who was full of death suddenly become full of life? When we're talking about our fellow Christians, that's what we're talking about—people who have been brought from death to life and from darkness into light by a merciful and miraculous act of God.

Do you realize that people are the masterpiece in God's creation? As you go through Genesis chapter 1, and you read about the days of creation, you see that on each day, God declared that it was good. But you get to the sixth day, which is the day in which man was created, and God says "it's very good." Do you get the implications of that? This is amazing! That means that He found more joy and pleasure in looking at humanity than He did in the most beautiful sunset or than He would on a night when you can see millions of stars in the sky.

The implication of all of this is that when you're talking about another believer, you're talking about someone whom God created and resurrected from the dead in a supernatural act that is **at least** as amazing as the very act of creating the universe in the beginning! See, the closer we get to thinking the way God thinks and seeing the way God sees, the more beauty and wonder we'll see in each of God's people. Would you rather look at a beautiful sunset or would you rather look at a fellow brother or sister in

Christ? If your answer is the sunset, don't worry . . . we're all a work in progress, and that means that you've got a ways to go, even if you're not there yet!

But the fact that a person doesn't see their fellow brothers and sisters in Christ the way that God does becomes apparent when that person doesn't love his fellow believers in a way that causes him to feel a sense of affection that resembles the way that Paul feels for the Philippians, and when someone doesn't love God's people that way, it's no wonder they feel more loyal to themselves than they are to a fellow group of believers (i.e., "a local church").

With all of that in mind, let's remember that this epistle—the letter to the Philippians—is about growing in our love for Jesus and our love for each other.

"And I am sure of this, that He who began a good work in you will bring it to completion at the day of Jesus Christ." (Philippians 1:6)

It is such a comfort to know that the completion of God's work doesn't hinge on us, isn't it? That's why I love this verse so much—add it to my proverbial list of favorites, because I find more assurance in these words than I could possibly hope to find within myself, my faithfulness to God, or my ability to do everything that He has called me to be and to do. In other words, I find no reason to find any hope if I don't look any further than the tip of my own nose.

You and I are like a painting that remains unfinished, and only the artist can see from the beginning what it will look like as a completed project. And when we're done, you'll have a masterpiece that is more beautiful and more amazing than you ever could have possibly imagined while the painting is in progress.

Likewise, Paul—knowing about the problems the Philippians were facing as a church—saw the church not as they were, but as he knew that they would be by the time that God was finished with them.

When preaching on this verse, Ray Stedman said, "Many times, I confess, in times of discouragement with myself when I utterly despaired of being what I ought to be, because I was so aware, as you must be at times, of the deceitfulness and subtlety of the flesh, that even when I want to be, I end up deceiving myself. I see the utter futility of depending on me to get this job done. Then I've remembered this verse."

God is at work, shaping and molding each and every one of us who are in Christ Jesus. He's teaching us, disciplining us, pruning us into the likeness of His Son. Sometimes we cooperate with that process, and sometimes we don't, and in those seasons, He teaches us and shapes us despite ourselves.

Imagine that there was a bridge that crossed over a vast chasm, and that upon inspection of the bridge, you noticed that all of the pillars were being supported by the strongest, most unbreakable granite. Yet, you spot one pillar midway across this bridge that is not built on granite. Rather, you find out that it's a pillar that is sculpted out of nothing but mud. And that pillar is supposed to bear the weight of this bridge. And as you look a little closer, you see that the mud is cracked and gradually chipping away. Who in their right mind would dare to cross such a bridge? Before you know it, that bridge will crack at its weakest point, and anyone who is ignorant, crazy, or stupid enough to try crossing the bridge will surely die in their efforts. And yet, this is what salvation would look like if it depended on us even a little bit. "On Christ, the solid Rock, I stand. All other ground is sinking sand."

One of the reasons that God guarantees that this work will be completed by Him is that His glory—His reputation—is invested in us, and it's at stake. There was a time when the wrath of God was about to fall on the Israelites because of the greatness of their sin. God says to Moses, "How long will this people despise me? And how long will they not believe in me, in spite of all the signs that I have done among them? I will strike them with the pestilence and disinherit them, and I will make of you a nation greater and mightier than they." And Moses intercedes for the Israelites, pleading with God:

"Now if you kill this people as one man, then the nations who have heard your fame will say, 'It is because the LORD was not <u>able</u> to bring this people into the land that he swore to give to them that he has killed them in the wilderness.'" (Numbers 14:15-16; underlining mine)

God's reputation was at stake among the nations, and Moses' desire is not so much for mercy as it is for what God's mercy will demonstrate. If God failed to deliver His people into the Promised Land, even if it was because of their own wretchedness, the nations would mock God for His failure to do what He originally set out to do. Moses' chief concern was for the glory of God, which is revealed in His greatest achievement, which is saving the weak and the wretched despite their flaws and failures.

But our God is a God who will complete what He begins, because it brings Him glory. What is impossible with men is possible with God.

There are those who would tell us that a person can walk away from this process. But given what Paul tells us in Romans 6 about how our old self was crucified with Christ (Romans 6:6), and what he says in Galatians about how "it is no longer I who live, but Christ who lives in me," the idea of us being able to walk away from God working on us is really as ridiculous as the idea of you or me raising the dead. Because that's the condition of the old nature that was replaced with a living nature when we became a new creation! It's wonderful to know that we can't walk away from this process by which God is working on us, and that He will be the One to bring us to completion when we stand before Jesus one day. Because if this process relies on us, even to the smallest extent, then we can't trust it. But the whole thing rests in His hands. We're each a work in progress—a masterpiece in the making . . . for now. But He will complete us and perfect us one day.

And sometimes, that's hard to imagine—sometimes especially in others, but even in ourselves. The challenge is to see others not as they are, but as what they are becoming, by the grace of God. And this is difficult. If you've ever gone through storms and trials where you felt like Peter falling into the sea the moment he took his eyes off of the Lord, you know what I'm talking about. We've probably all felt that way about ourselves at some point or another. That's why, the moment we receive some kind of compliment, we think that the person giving the compliment must be missing how flawed we are! And I think that the Philippians would have too. And so Paul writes:

"It is right for me to feel this way about you all, because I hold you in my heart, for you are all partakers with me of grace, both in my imprisonment and in the defense and

confirmation of the gospel. For God is my witness, how I yearn for you all with the affection of Christ Jesus."
(Philippians 1:7-8)

See, there's a pretty good chance that the moment that Paul started talking about how much joy he felt as he remembered them in prayer, and how he was sure that God is going to complete the work that He began in them, they would have reacted by feeling like they didn't deserve such praise and accolades. Not from a guy like Paul (at least in their minds). That's the reaction that Paul is expecting from them, and so he immediately starts defending the affection and the love that he has for them. He's basically saying, "No, really; this really is how I should feel about you!" Why? For the same reason that we should love our fellow brothers and sisters in Christ: we are partakers of the same grace, and by that grace, we have all been adopted into the same family.

And this is how Paul feels about ALL of the Christians in Philippi. It's important that he says that, because it erases any boundaries that may have been drawn within the church by those who were causing division. Paul feels this love toward every single one of them; even the ones who were causing problems.

And the secret to how he does that is revealed in verse 8. His love for them is more than an emotional experience. It's the affection that Jesus has toward His people that Paul is experiencing. How can one hold animosity against someone or ill will toward someone whom Christ gave His life to redeem? The closer our heart is to God's, the more we love what He loves and hate what He hates. And friends, God loves His people. And so when we refuse to make the choice to love His people, what we're doing is creating a distance between our heart and His.

Paul's love for them flowed out of the unity that God desires for His people to have. Remember that Jesus prayed that we would be one, as He and the Father are one (John 17:11). And the way we do that is by making a conscious and deliberate choice to love one another, flaws and all. To make that easier, remember that the same God whom you profess to love and who dwells within you also dwells within them. How does He see them? Because if we see them differently than He does, then it's our own selfishness and stubbornness that's preventing us from seeing others as God does. Something amazing happens when we learn to see other Christians the way that God sees them: we become more amazed and find greater awe in the fact that God loves us! And the more wonder and awe we find in that, the more we love Him. And the more we love Him, the more easily we learn to love others in the way that He does. And that's how Paul or anyone grows in affection toward his fellow Christians—even the ones who are difficult to love.

The person who refuses to love and be reconciled with their brothers or sisters in Christ is in a dark and dangerous place. This helps to explain why John says that the person who hates (that is, refuses to make the choice to love) his brother or sister in Christ cannot love God (1st John 4:20).

As we get deeper into this study, we'll find more keys to learning how to love one another better and more like Jesus. But for now, Paul continues sharing his heartfelt prayers for the Philippians, writing:

"And it is my prayer that your love may abound more and more, with knowledge and all discernment, so that you may approve what is excellent, and so be pure and blameless for the day of Christ, filled with the fruit of righteousness that

comes through Jesus Christ, to the glory and praise of
God." (Philippians 1:9-11)

Notice something here with me: when Paul says that he
prays that their love may abound more and more, what,
specifically does he mean? In other words, what is the
object of that love? He leaves us wondering, doesn't he?
But the hint that he leaves is how their love will abound
more and more. First, it will abound because of knowledge.
Knowledge of what? Maybe the better question is:
knowledge of whom? Knowledge of God, undoubtedly.
Paul knew that the more they learned about God and
learned about His ways, the more they would experience—
both individually and collectively—a stronger sense of love
and fellowship toward one another.

But he also knows that discernment will cause their love to
abound. The word "discernment" means to perceive
without sight and to hear without sound. It means engaging
the mind, the intellect. It means understanding. In the
context that Paul is using the word, it means "learning to
gain spiritual insight."

One of the great dividers of people is a failure to discern
intention and meaning. And so there's a failure to
understand one another fully, because one person will make
a comment or two, and the other person, who cannot
discern what they meant, interprets it to mean something
totally different from what was intended. Now, someone
who is mature will go to that person privately if they feel
offended by their understanding of what was said, and
they'll try to clear the air. But this is not only difficult, but
it doesn't always work, because it takes two people who are
committed to loving each other no matter what, and the fact
of the matter is that there are plenty of people who don't

have that commitment toward their fellow brothers and sisters in Christ. And that, dear friends, is absolutely tragic.

And so Paul prays that they would grow in their love for God and for each other because they were growing in their ability to discern or understand one another and to perceive the needs that others had. Love always seeks to do what is best, but figuring out what is best is not always easy. That's where discernment becomes crucial.

But I think that there's another way that abounding in love is aided by our ability to discern, and that is to discern the prompting of the Holy Spirit. He's going to prompt us to do things that make us uncomfortable sometimes. And the more a person refuses to follow those promptings, the less able they are to discern when He's prompting us to act. And this involves a long and difficult learning process.

I think of how a pet is taught to discern her master's commands. Dogs don't know to sit when we say "sit" without some training, but once the master works with her for a while, she'll be able to discern commands like "sit," "lay down," or "stay." The Master is working on us, and the more we learn to discern His promptings, leading, and guiding, the more obedient we'll be, and the more we'll abound in love—both for God and for our brothers and sisters in Christ.

When we have knowledge and discernment, Paul tells us that we'll be able to approve of what is excellent. Because we are in Christ Jesus, you and I should have very different ideas than the world does of what constitutes "excellence." What does it mean for something to be excellent? It's referring to the things in life that matter most. If you were to ask the most mature and truly devoted Christian what matters most, there is a short list of answers that you could expect to hear: "God is excellent." "The Bible is excellent." "Meeting regularly as a church to study the word of God is excellent." But if you ask someone who is not a Christian what matters most, you can expect a wide range of answers. Maybe they'll say "success" or "happiness" or "sex" or "tolerance," but these are people who do not desire the things of God. They neither know Him nor do they discern His will. If they did, they would change the way that they live!

When our lives feel chaotic or like they're spinning out of control, we have this tendency of taking our eyes off of the things that matter most, and we revert to seeing things as the world sees things. And when that happens, we see someone backslide into sin. Why? Because we love being in control! But the reality is that if you are in Christ, your life is never out of control; it's just out of your control. And sometimes (maybe even often times), that's a really good thing. If it feels like life is out of control, and that causes us to fear, which causes us to take our eyes off of the things that matter most, it's ultimately because our love is not being driven by knowledge and discernment. Rather, when it feels like our lives are out of our control, it probably gets driven more by emotions than anything else, which can lead us all over the place. And thus we tend to start approving of things that are not excellent.

The Christian who lacks a love that is driven by both knowledge and discernment will not be demonstrating obedience to the Lord, and thus will not be abounding in love toward God or toward their brothers and sisters in Christ the way that they should be.

When our love is driven by knowledge and discernment, we will approve of what is excellent, and when we approve of what is excellent, Paul tells us that we'll be pure and blameless for the day of Christ. In other words, we'll be living in a way that says, "I'm ready for Jesus to return whenever He's ready."

The Greek word that gets translated as "pure" here is very interesting. It can also be translated more literally as "judged" or "revealed by the light of the sun." In other words, there's nothing that has gone unchecked. The light is shining so that our lives are open to full and thorough examination. The way that a person in the ancient world would check to see if a vessel could be trusted to hold water was to hold it up to the sunlight and see if a crack could be spotted. So what Paul is saying is that when we've got our priorities lined up straight, approving of what is excellent by God's understanding of what is excellent, it can stand up to the most thorough examination possible, because our lives will be filled with what Paul calls "fruits of righteousness."

Paul tells us that the fruit of the Spirit is love, joy, peace, patience, kindness, goodness, faithfulness, gentleness, and self-control. These are things that we will not learn—not even in the slightest degree—by the force of our willpower. Rather, as we learn to discern the voice of the Holy Spirit whispering in our ear, prompting us, guiding us, and leading us, we will grow in these qualities.

The presence of Jesus in our lives and the work that He has done and continues to do on our lives enables us to live rightly before Him. The righteousness that we live out is evidence of Him continuing His work in our lives. If you desire assurance of salvation with God, do not look to the past to some decision that you've made. Look to the present. Look at what's most important to you right now, and look for fruits of righteousness in your life right now. Assurance is found in looking back on our lives and seeing how our desires are becoming more and more conformed to the things that God desires. Our sanctification is proof of our justification.

Are you living to the glory and praise of God in such a way that people can't help but see your love or your joy or the other fruit of the Spirit? That's good fruit, which Paul tells us only comes through a relationship with Jesus Christ. Through this relationship, we learn to live our lives with an outward focus—focused on God and His people, rather than on ourselves.

J.C. Ryle said this: "Let your Christianity be so unmistakable, your eye so single, your heart so whole, your walk so straightforward that all who see you may have no doubt whose you are and whom you serve." By His great love for us, He extends grace to us so that we can always come to Him and confess our flaws and failures—whether that be not loving Him rightly or not loving our fellow Christians rightly—and know that His grace is enough. The grace that gave us new life is the same grace that sustains us constantly in our standing before God. We cannot bear that weight. Just like He sustains the universe, and the universe would dissipate into nothingness if He stopped sustaining it, so too the faith of the believer would be forever lost if God were not sustaining it by His grace. And His grace is always sufficient to keep us growing with knowledge and discernment in our love for Him and for His people.

To grow in our walk with Him means to be abounding in that love, because we're abiding in the One who is the foundation of our salvation and our source of life. Our knowledge of Him and our ability to discern His leading in our lives will guide the choices that we make, both with Him and with one another, and when that's happening, we're desiring what He is and what He wants so much that on the day that we stand before Him, we'll desire only Him and we'll want nothing to do with anything which distracts us from pursuing and desiring Him, because we'll be abounding in love for Him. And when we are abounding in love for God and for His people, it brings praise and glory to the God who will one day complete the work He began in us.

~~~

Chapter 3: Unshackled Joy

Philippians 1:12-20

There was an interesting study that was done on Olympians a few years back at the 2010 Winter Olympics: they surveyed people who had won medals to gauge their level of excitement. One would rightfully expect someone who wins a gold medal to be feeling the most joy, and indeed, the study revealed that the gold medalist feels more joy about receiving a medal than either the silver or bronze medal recipients. But which medal do you think felt the second most joyful to receive a medal? One might expect the answer to be the silver medalist, but what this study revealed was that bronze medalists tend to feel significantly more joyful about winning a medal than silver medalists feel.

There are probably a variety of possible reasons that silver medalists feel less joy than bronze medalists, but it seems at least reasonable to assume that a silver medalist thinks to themselves, "Ah, I was so close to winning the gold!" And so the medal feels more like a consolation prize. A bronze medalist, on the other hand, is likely thinking, "Man, I almost didn't get a medal!" And so they're just thankful to get a medal at all!

This is actually a common phenomenon. Psychologists call it "counter-factual thinking," and it involves that little voice in our head that keeps saying, "I could have done this" or "I should have done that." Personally, I think it's appropriate to call it "second place syndrome." And if you look at our culture over-all, you see "second place syndrome" all over the place. It's ironic ,because we have the highest standards of living in human history, and yet it's never enough. The irony is that while we have all of this luxury in our society, we're simultaneously a culture that is facing an epidemic of depression that's greater than the world has ever seen. You can try to explain that however you want, but I think that the answer is pretty simple: people try to find joy in things and in circumstances, and when your joy is contingent upon your material possessions or your circumstances or on anything else that can give way under your feet at any moment, your life will have little or no true joy.

As we started our study on Paul's letter to the church in Philippi, we saw that Paul was absolutely overflowing with joy as he remembered them and consistently held them up in prayer. And this was his attitude despite the fact that he was chained to a Roman guard as he wrote this letter. That doesn't seem like ideal circumstances, does it? Of course not. In fact, one might think that feeling "second place syndrome" would be justified and reasonable in Paul's case, wouldn't they? I mean, nobody could really be excited about being imprisoned, could they?

Let's look at what Paul has to say as we continue in this study.

"I want you to know, brothers, that what has happened to me has really served to advance the gospel, so that it has become known throughout the whole imperial guard and to all the rest that my imprisonment is for Christ. And most of the brothers, having become confident in the Lord by my imprisonment, are much more bold to speak the word without fear." (Philippians 1:12-14)

Here's the secret of Paul's joy: first of all, it's not based on his circumstances. Well, what's it based on? The obvious answer is that Paul finds his joy in Jesus, but upon closer examination, we find another reason which is related to the first: Paul isn't feeling joy because of his circumstances as much as he's finding joy in the **opportunities** that his circumstances are bringing to him.

Now, just to be honest, I would probably at least be tempted to see the opportunity to write this letter as an opportunity to air my grievances against those who are limiting my mobility. Maybe I'd complain about how harshly I was being treated, or about how much I hate going to the bathroom with a Roman guard chained to me. Maybe I'd complain about the fact that I wasn't being fed nearly enough. And if this is what you got from me, it would be completely obvious to everyone that I wasn't feeling joy, because my words would be a reflection of the fact that I didn't like my circumstances. But that's not what we see in Paul. He probably had every reason to complain, but he was choosing instead to remain focused on reasons to rejoice, starting with the fact that because of his imprisonment, the gospel was advancing!

One of the things that people love to ask is how we can know where God wants us to be. And we see people get ridiculously superstitious about this kind of thing. The last place we think God would want us to be is in a bad situation, right? But Paul sees that this bad situation that he's in is exactly where God wants him to be. How does he know that? Because that's where he is as he writes this! To believe otherwise is a pretty small, limited view of God.

Have you ever turned the whole thing around on yourself like that when you're in the midst of a trial or difficult circumstance? That takes trust, but isn't that what the whole Bible is ultimately directing us to do? To trust in God? You could summarize every single book in the Bible that way. What's the book of Exodus about? Trusting God. What's the book of Job about? Trusting God. What's the book of Revelation about? No, it's not about how to survive or predict the end of the world. The book of Revelation is about trusting God. See, the book of Revelation is important because it tells us that Jesus isn't done with His work on earth. If there was no book of Revelation, we'd go through the Old Testament and say, "Oh wait . . . the Messiah was supposed to establish an everlasting Kingdom, and He was supposed to bring peace and defeat Satan." And the book of Revelation assures us that Jesus will do everything that the Bible says He will do. So trust God!

The more a person trusts in God, the more we see something amazing happen: they find their greatest joy in Jesus, because He's becoming their greatest treasure, and so their joy is undeterred through difficult circumstances, because they know that Jesus knows all about difficult circumstances. He can sympathize with our weakness, our pain, our suffering, and our trials.

He told His disciples, "Consider the lilies, how they grow: they neither toil nor spin, yet I tell you, even Solomon in all his glory was not arrayed like one of these. But if God so clothes the grass, which is alive in the field today, and tomorrow is thrown into the oven, how much more will he clothe you, O you of little faith! And do not seek what you are to eat and what you are to drink, nor be worried. For all the nations of the world seek after these things, and your Father knows that you need them. Instead, seek His kingdom, and these things will be added to you" (Luke 12:27-31). What's the kingdom? Jesus is the kingdom.

That's why Jesus said, "The Kingdom of God is at hand—repent and believe the Gospel" (Mark 1:15).

So what was Jesus teaching His disciples? He was teaching them that when they're tempted to worry and fret about their situation or about not having enough of this or that, seek Him—seek Jesus—and know that He'll provide what we need. In other words: "Trust God!"

Not one person on the face of the earth can die before God says it's time, so it's not like they're going to die . . . unless the Lord says that it's their time to come home!

Knowing that wherever we are and whatever our circumstances may be are in God's hands frees us up to find joy in Him, because we trust Him as our all-powerful, all-good, sovereign God, and we know that He's always working out the circumstances for our greatest good, teaching us to become like Jesus. Sometimes that happens in trials by fire, and sometimes it happens in seasons of rest.

The main thing I want us to see here is that Paul's attitude regarding his circumstances was his circumstances were serving a holy and righteous purpose: the spreading of the Gospel. Do you see the irony here? Paul can't advance, but despite the fact that he can't (or maybe because he can't), the Gospel can. Do you know what this all boils down to? When life gives you lemons, make lemonade.

We can be certain that the guard who was chained to Paul was hearing the Gospel, and Paul tells us that the whole imperial guard was getting a taste of it. The imperial guard refers to the special military unit which served as bodyguards for Caesar. Paul wasn't intimidated in the least by these guys who were sworn to protect Caesar! See, the chains which shackled him would have been viewed by the guards as evidence of Caesar's power over Paul. But in Paul's case, the chains were evidence of Christ's power and lordship in his life.

Imagine the first conversation he had with the guard he was chained to. He turns to Paul and says, "Are you in chains for disobeying our lord?" He's referring to Caesar. And Paul responds, "To the contrary, I'm in chains because of my obedience to the Lord--the Lord Jesus. Have you heard of Jesus? He is the incarnate God who came to bear the wrath of God against our sins, so that His righteousness was transferred to us while our sin was transferred to Him. Yes, friend, He died to reconcile you and me and anyone who believes in Him to God. You can be forgiven! And He rose again three days later to prove it! And one day, every knee will bow and every tongue will confess that He is Lord of all—either with their will or against it." "What? Even Caesar?" "Yes, even Caesar." If you know anything about Paul, you know that his answer would have been something like that. See, because of Paul's circumstances, these Gentiles who were serving as Caesar's bodyguards were hearing the Gospel. They wouldn't have heard it otherwise! Not only that, but Paul tells us that the preaching of the Gospel message was increasing as a result of his imprisonment. They're saying, "That's so awesome! I wish I had the chance to do that!" And so what are they doing? They're going out and speaking with even more boldness than they had before!

The point in all of this is that our circumstances are not as important as what we do with them! "Whatever you do, do all for the glory of God" (1st Cor. 10:31). If you find joy in bringing glory to God, the possibilities for finding joy in even the hardest circumstances are only limited by our desire to see God glorified and our obedience to what He has called us to do. If you find joy in bringing glory to God, the possibilities for finding joy in any situation are limitless!

Ironically, sometimes we may even find more joy in our grief than we do in happiness. This is one of those places where we find the power of God, which meets us and comforts us in our weakness and in our hardships and trials.

Do not confuse joy and happiness. While they are similar, the Bible does not use those words interchangeably; they are distinct from one another. See, happiness is a feeling, but joy is a choice. Joy can certainly lead to happiness, but joy is a decision that we make which stems from a deep trust in God. In order for us to experience abundant, overflowing joy, we must make a deliberate choice to find our greatest treasure in Jesus. Was Paul tempted to feel sorry for himself? I am sure he was. But he chose to keep his mind focused on Jesus rather than his situation. This is Paul's attitude. He is shackled, but his joy is not. We would do well to follow his example.

Apparently, some people thought that Paul's experience was so amazing that it was causing rivalry.

"Some indeed preach Christ from envy and rivalry, but others from good will. The latter do it out of love, knowing that I am put here for the defense of the gospel. The former proclaim Christ out of selfish ambition, not sincerely but thinking to afflict me in my imprisonment. What then? Only that in every way, whether in pretense or in truth, Christ is proclaimed, and in that I rejoice." (Philippians 1:15-18a)

Isn't this interesting? Paul's not talking about Judaizers or other types of false teachers here. We know how Paul feels about those who teach a false Gospel. This is the same Paul who said of those who taught the requirement of circumcision, "I wish those who unsettle you would emasculate themselves" (Galatians 5:12). Paul got angry about anyone who convoluted or distorted the Gospel in any way, but he's not angry here. Why? Because he's talking about people who are proclaiming the true Gospel—the same one that got Paul beaten so many times and thrown in prison.

Who are these people? Paul tells us that there are two types, based on personal motives. First, there are those who are preaching the Gospel because they envy or oppose Paul. They rival him. They don't rejoice in his success in advancing the Gospel. These are people who are responding to Paul's imprisonment out of selfish ambition. These are not necessarily people who were rejoicing over Paul's imprisonment. Rather, these are people who hated the fact that Paul was imprisoned because he was gaining a reputation for his faithful preaching because of it. They didn't hate it because they loved Paul—they hated it because they loved themselves! They were probably hearing from other Christians about how much Paul was accomplishing in terms of the Gospel advancing despite his imprisonment, and so they were preaching the Gospel boldly themselves in order that they would impress others with their fearlessness and boldness.

So did this first group, who preached the Gospel out of a motivation of envy and rivalry, get under Paul's skin at all? Not at all. Why? Because even though their motives weren't pure, their message was. How wild is this? Someone with an impure heart can preach a pure message. This is one of the wonders of preaching: every messenger is flawed. Every one of us sins, makes mistakes, and has plenty of weaknesses. And yet, God can and does use the words of the messenger to stir a sinner's heart toward repentance and righteousness.

What a magnificent thing it is to know that God can work to save the unregenerate in spite of the personal flaws and weaknesses of the messenger! That takes a lot of weight off of our shoulders, because the work of regeneration belongs to Him. Apart from God softening the ears of the hearer, it doesn't matter how close to perfect the messenger might seem, either in terms of his actions or how polished up his Gospel presentation is.

Now, Paul is keenly aware of their motivation, but he's also aware of the message that they're proclaiming. And so he rejoices over it. This is one of the signs of a mature believer—they rejoice at the success that others are having; even if those others don't like them for whatever reason! Again, finding this kind of joy requires looking beyond our circumstances and focusing on what really matters. And for Paul, the spreading of the Gospel and the glorification of God mattered most. Everything else was just details that were ultimately insignificant.

One last word about these people who were acting out of envy and rivalry: don't miss the fact that that's one of the issues that the church in Philippi was facing. So what we see here is that, once again, Paul is teaching by example. Rather than getting bent out of shape about someone having success or influence, rejoice that the Gospel message is being proclaimed! Rejoice over the success of anyone whom God is using to accomplish that purpose!

The second group of people who are those who are preaching from what Paul calls "good will." Paul says here in verse 16 that their motivation is love. They knew that Paul was in prison because of a noble cause: preaching and defending the Gospel. And when Paul was imprisoned, they realized that someone needed to step up and take Paul's place, because the proclamation of the Gospel needed to go on. They knew that this is what Paul would have wanted them to do, and so they weren't preaching out of selfish ambition or to rival Paul; they preached to support and stand beside Paul.

Either way, as long as the Gospel was being preached, Paul rejoiced. And if his own personal imprisonment caused more people to do it (which seems to have been one of the effects of his imprisonment), then all the more glory to God!

Paul hasn't said much about how he's feeling about what's to come for him, but he now takes a moment to share his outlook and his attitude with the Philippians, writing:

"Yes, and I will rejoice, for I know that through your prayers and the help of the Spirit of Jesus Christ this will turn out for my deliverance, as it is my eager expectation and hope that I will not be at all ashamed, but that with full courage now as always Christ will be honored in my body, whether by life or by death." (Philippians 1:18b-20)

Those in the Philippian church who were familiar with the book of Job may have caught the reference that Paul was making here, because the Greek word that is translated "deliverance" also means "salvation." In Job 13:16, we read Job say, "This will be my salvation: that the godless shall not come before Him." Of course, Job was a man who was righteous. In fact, he was the most righteous person on the face of the planet in his day. And yet he suffered greatly, not in spite of his faith, but **because** of it.

This is just one of the areas where the Word of Faith/Prosperity gospel gets it so incredibly wrong. Prosperity teaching is not just a misunderstanding or a mis-application of Scripture. It is so far off from the truth, I believe that there is a dishonest element to it. Job's suffering was due to his righteousness, but the Prosperity message teaches that if you have enough faith, you'll never suffer. Nothing could be further from the truth! The more righteous and faithful you are, the more likely you are to encounter trials and tribulations, and Paul realizes that he's an example of that principle in action.

Paul has confidence in his ultimate deliverance. Look at the verb that he uses in verse 19. He says, "I **know** that this will turn out for my deliverance" (emphasis added). He didn't say "I hope" or "I wish." He is confident that this will result in his deliverance. Similarly, he doesn't say, "I hope (or wish) that Christ would be honored in my body, whether by life or by death;" he says "Christ **will be** honored!"

It seems apparent to me that Paul has wrestled his way through this issue, and he's come to terms with his situation. Just like Job concludes that he will be delivered from his trials in one way or another, Paul is 100% confident that whether he lives or dies, Christ will be magnified and exalted. And this fact—that Christ will be exalted—is the deliverance he's talking about. He's not talking about going free. He doesn't know if he's going to be released. What he means is that his defense of the Gospel and his proclamation of the Gospel will not be for nothing.

Paul knows that he's ultimately going to have to stand trial before Nero. Do you know who Nero is? He's the one who fed Christians to the lions. He's the one who sent the

Roman army in to pillage the temple of Jerusalem, as well as the rest of the city. And he ended up having it all burned to the ground. Nero absolutely hated Christians. In fact, if you were to make a list of the top 10 people throughout history who have hated and persecuted Christians, Nero's name would probably be somewhere toward the top of that list.

In spite of his impending trial, no matter what happens, Paul will be vindicated because his greatest desire will be fulfilled regardless of the outcome. What's his greatest desire? That God would be glorified. He can't control the outcome in terms of whether he lives or dies, and so he doesn't worry about it. What he can do is make sure that whatever happens, Christ is exalted. And so he's sure of that much, and that's a good enough for rejoicing for him.

Now this deliverance that he is so confident in will come because of two things: first of all, he says, through the prayers of his fellow brothers and sisters in Christ. Has anyone ever believed in the power of intercessory prayer as strongly as Paul did? I doubt it! He constantly prayed for others, and constantly sought the prayers of others. That's one request he frequently made in his letters. Why was intercessory prayer so important to him? Because he'd seen the fruit of intercessory prayer firsthand, and so he knew that prayer made a difference. This wasn't just any battle they were facing. Ultimately, it was spiritual warfare. Paul wasn't afraid of Nero; he was afraid of the one before whom he would stand and give an account for his life one day. And so the prayers of God's people gave him confidence.

Secondly, he's confident that his suffering will not be for naught because he knows that the Spirit of Jesus Christ will help him. Of course, here Paul is referring to the Holy

Spirit. Remember that Jesus promised that if He went away to the Father, He would ask the Father who would send another. Another what? Another helper, according to John 14:16. But it's very interesting that Paul uses this word that gets translated as "help." Literally, what it means is "supply." So what Paul's saying is that he's confident that the Holy Spirit will supply him with whatever he needs—not with what he wants, but with what he needs—to stand strong for the Gospel.

Paul was confident that his trials would glorify Christ, and that he would be sustained by the prayers of his brothers and sisters in Christ and the empowering presence of the Holy Spirit in his life. He hopes that he won't be ashamed—that is, "put to shame." But even if he is, even though it's not ideal or something that Paul necessarily desired, Christ can still be exalted and glorified. Was he going to be humiliated for his proclamation of the Gospel? Maybe. Maybe not. He hoped not, but he knew that he could face anything because of these two pillars of support upon which he stood.

I think that one of the reasons we often fail to show the boldness that Paul had in preaching the Gospel can be attributed to a couple of things. First of all, we struggle to choose to feel joy despite our circumstances. We love to feel happy because of our circumstances, because that feels more natural. But if that's what we need to feel joy, then we're not in control of our joy. In that case, it's not a fruit of the Spirit working in our lives; it's the fruit of our circumstances, and it will just kind of come and go, because life isn't always exactly what we hope for or expect.

But the second reason that we often fail to demonstrate Paul's boldness is that we want to have a boldness that's rooted in ourselves and our confidence or ability to do something. But here's the thing: we can't do anything good on our own. That's why Jesus said, "Abide in me, and I in you. As the branch cannot bear fruit by itself, unless it abides in the vine, neither can you, unless you abide in Me. I am the vine; you are the branches. Whoever abides in me and I in him, he it is that bears much fruit, for apart from me you can do nothing." (John 15:4-5).

Do not base your confidence in yourself—base your confidence in the fact that you will bear good fruit for Christ if you are abiding in Him. What does it mean to abide in Him? It means to do His will and keep Him at the forefront of our minds. It means that Jesus isn't just someone we idealize or sing to on Sunday mornings (He's all that and more), but that He's the person we live every second of every day for. It means that nothing takes priority in our lives over Him—nothing!

When we do that—when we learn to abide in Jesus—we will not only bear good fruit, but we will also find every reason in the world to find joy in Him, no matter what our circumstances may be, because His glory is what we desire the most! Circumstances will try to rob us of our joy and shake our confidence in God and distract us, but let us live for Christ in the face of any and every circumstance, and find unshakeable comfort and joy in Him.

This is a call to surrender to Jesus every circumstance that would hinder us or undo us, and every distraction that would prevent us from desiring Him above all things, in order that He would be glorified in us, no matter what our circumstances may be.

~~~

Chapter 4: To Live is Christ, To Die is Gain

Philippians 1:21-24

One of the questions that every philosopher since the dawn of humanity has asked is "What is the meaning of life?" This is a question that goes back thousands upon thousands of years, and there are so many different answers, one could spend their lifetime exploring all of the various answers to the question. So it's entirely possible that when asked about the meaning of life, they could answer, "To explore every possible answer to that question" or "to read every answer to that question that Google can possibly find." And you probably really could spend your lifetime on a task like that.

Let's take a quick look at how some well-known writers and philosophers have responded to this question.

"To be what we are, and to become what we are capable of becoming, is the only end of life." (Robert Louis Stevenson)

"Life has to be given a meaning because of the obvious fact that it has no meaning." (Henry Miller)

"The Ultimate Answer to Life, The Universe and Everything is...42!" (Douglas Adams)

"The purpose of life is to stay alive. Watch any animal in nature--all it tries to do is stay alive. It doesn't care about beliefs or philosophy." (Michael Crighton)

"Life is meaningless, when we take a life we take nothing of value." (Brent Weeks)

The truth is that for a lot of modern writers and thinkers, life has no ultimate meaning. Steve Martin is now a famous comedian, but he started out as a student of philosophy at California State University, Long Beach. And once he started exploring this question, he too arrived at the conclusion that life is meaningless, and therefore, he concluded, we should just laugh as much as possible. He said, "In philosophy, I started studying logic, and they were talking about cause and effect, and you start to realize, 'Hey, there is no cause and effect! There is no logic! There is no anything!'" (Fong-Torres, Ben (1982) "Steve Martin Sings: The Rolling Stone Interview". *Rolling Stone* February 18, 1982. Issue 363).

I would take issue with that. I don't know how many classes he took in philosophy or which philosophers he studied, but this idea that life is meaningless is something that only modern philosophers have arrived at. In fact, the idea that life is meaningless really started to take off around the same time that the idea of evolution started being tossed around. How ironic. Coincidence? Probably not.

With that fact in mind, we'd do well to remember that even Solomon repeatedly affirmed, "All is vanity" or "everything is meaningless" throughout the book of Ecclesiastes. That is, he affirms it until he reaches the end of the book, where he reveals that the only things that have true meaning are things which are done out of obedience to

God. Indeed, apart from God, life has no meaning or purpose. And life is so incredibly short.

Let's take a quick look at some of the things aside from God that people make their lives about, and you'll see what I mean.

A person can feel like their job gives their life meaning. But that's really just an illusion, because, first of all, a person can lose their job in a heartbeat; where or what is a person's identity based on when they're jobless? But secondly, this idea sets a person up for a miserable life, because no matter how good you are at your job, you could always do better. And so even if you find meaning, a person has to realize that their life didn't have as much meaning as it could have, if they had only been better at their job.

A person can feel like their material things give their life meaning. But again, it's an illusion, because it can all be gone in a heartbeat. The things we own today aren't coming with us to the grave.

A person can feel like fame gives their life meaning. But again, that can be here today and gone tomorrow, and fame is a fragile thing—it's never stagnant, and it can't continue increasing indefinitely. There's going to reach a point where it declines, and then what? Life has less and less meaning?

A person can feel like life is about being entertained, but it's never enough: eventually we get bored with being entertained.

And don't live for beauty either, because this mixture of gravity and age gets the best of every single one of us.

Hopefully you get the point. The things of this world don't make our lives meaningful. Not in the least bit. And yet every single one of us is living for something. Even the philosophers and writers who assert that life is meaningless spend their lives trying to fill their lives with some sort of purpose or meaning. There are no exceptions—every person on the face of the earth looks for meaning in something, and that's revealed in what they devote their lives to. The real question is whether or not the thing(s) we live for are worth dying for. Because if the things that we find meaning in aren't worth dying for, how could they possibly be worth living for?

What's Paul's answer to this question? He writes this:

"For to me to live is Christ, and to die is gain."
(Philippians 1:21)

While others would say, "to live is work," or "to live is finding fame," or "to live is _____ (fill in the blank)", these answers are all lacking, because those things don't bring gain in death. Rather, they bring tremendous loss in death. In fact, I would be so bold as to say that any answer other than what Paul has declared here is the same as saying that life is meaningless.

Paul's life was so transformed by the gospel! Through him, and through anyone whose life is or was dedicated to the glory of God and the spreading of the gospel, we see that the gospel does so much more than just change our standing before God. Friends, everyone wants to have a good standing before God. There isn't an unbelieving person on the face of the planet who isn't just kind of hoping for the best once this life is over and done with. For the atheist, the hope is literally for their existence to evaporate into nothingness, rather than being confronted with the reality that they have willfully and deliberately refused to believe in the One who could save them from the wrath of God against their sin. "For what can be known about God is plain to them, because God has shown it to them," but in their unrighteousness, they have very intentionally suppressed the very truth that could have saved them (Romans 1:18-19).

The gospel changes everything. It starts by changing our nature through God's act of regeneration, and it simultaneously changes our standing before God. But then it continues changing us—changing our attitudes and our values. Why else would Paul write his most joyful letter while chained to a member of the Roman Imperial Guard?

The gospel also changes the meaningfulness of our lives. While we were once enemies of God who lived for nothing and nobody but ourselves, by faith in Jesus Christ and repentance we were adopted as orphans into God's family, which freed us to live for things which have eternal significance—in other words, to live for things that truly have meaning. So the atheist, godless writers and philosophers are correct in what they have found: life has no meaning for them. But they haven't exactly turned over every stone, have they? And if they have intentionally avoided turning over the one stone that has the answer, which is precisely what the Scriptures affirm they have done, how can they claim to be wise? Romans 1:22 gives us the answer: "Professing to be wise, they became fools."

So what does it mean to live for Jesus? I think that Jesus answered this question very succinctly in one sentence. In Matthew 13:44, He says this:

"The kingdom of heaven is like treasure hidden in a field, which a man found and covered up. Then in his joy he goes and sells all that he has and buys that field."

So the Kingdom of Heaven is like a treasure. What is the Kingdom of Heaven? Again, Jesus is the Kingdom of Heaven. So Jesus is like a treasure hidden in a field. What does it cost this hypothetical man (who represents you, me, or anyone else) to buy that field? Everything. Do you get the impression that there was anything in this man's life— anything that he possessed, anything that he wanted to possess, or anything that he valued—that he wasn't willing to completely abandon for the sake of having the treasure in this field? No, Jesus tells us that he was joyful to give everything up for the sake of having this field.

The question that we're forced to ask ourselves here is: "What do I desire to have more than Jesus? What am I holding on to that I would not joyfully give up for the sake of knowing and being known by Jesus?" Because if there is anything that you can think of—even your own life— that you wouldn't let go of or give a lower priority to than Jesus, then you have to wonder if you have the assurance of owning this proverbial field.

So whatever it is that you're living for, this is a picture of what it really is in comparison to the incredible glory and blessing of gaining Christ. What this comparison really boils down to is a choice to either live for Christ or to live for "rubbish." As Matt Chandler puts it, "When everything considered valuable in life is seen to be nothing in comparison to the glory of Christ, you learn rather well that Christ alone is worth living for" (Chandler, To Live is Christ, To Die is Gain).

Friend, the question is not whether or not you believe in God. The question is not even if you want to go to heaven when you die. The question is: what would you not completely surrender to Jesus in order to have Him? I am personally begging every one of you to be completely honest about this question, and I would ask that if there is anything that you would refuse to release in order to have Jesus (even your own life, even your family), please surrender it. Please rearrange your priorities and values, because the child of God who has disorganized priorities (i.e., putting anything before Jesus) is eventually going to be disciplined. Trust me—I've been there and done that, because I insisted on learning the hard way. And if you love something more than Jesus but don't get disciplined . . . I think we all know the implications of that. So with fear and trembling, please see that the treasure of gaining Jesus is worth more than anything else, and that you cannot gain Him if you value anything else more than you value Him. Please—I am begging you to understand and know how incredibly important this is. But rest assured that the blessing of being redeemed and known by Jesus more than compensates the true believer for anything and everything they have sacrificed for the sake of following and glorifying Him.

The question "What is the meaning of life?" is actually the first question that the Westminster Shorter Catechism offers an answer to. It poses the question right off the bat, "What is the chief end of man?" The "chief end" is just a fancy way of saying "meaning" or "purpose." That's the language that they used in 1647. The answer: "Man's chief end is to glorify God, and to enjoy him for ever." If you want to find true, lasting purpose in life, you must learn to live in and for Christ Jesus.

This is the whole experience of Christian living. Four words: "to live is Christ." Paul gives us a wonderful summary of what it means to live for Christ in the next verse:

"If I am to live in the flesh, that means fruitful labor for me. Yet which I shall choose I cannot tell." (Philippians 1:22)

How many people can truly say that? He's saying that if he had to choose to live or die, he's not sure which he would prefer. He's saying that he sees his imprisonment, his impending trial before Nero, and the possibility of him being put to death as a win-win proposition. The only thing that could make an attitude like Paul's possible was to have Jesus as the source, the center, the power, and the purpose of his life—and every single one of us who is in Christ can find freedom to live above and beyond the ordinary and common life by being transformed and empowered by Jesus in the same way.

Notice that this isn't just some internal faith or devotion that he keeps hidden away and private. I'm certain that he has an inward devotion and a private walk with Jesus, but it overflows into his actions. That's why he refers to this as living "in the flesh." His fruitful labor is plentiful, but it's an outward reflection of something that is an internal reality for Paul—that reality being that he was passionate about living for the glory and exaltation of Jesus Christ.

Following Jesus means denying one's self, taking up our cross, and walking the same path that Jesus walked (Mark 8:34). When our purpose for living is found in Christ— when He alone is the answer to our questions about the meaning of life—one of the things that will inevitably happen is that we follow in Christ's path. We learn to love what He loves, and we learn to do what He did. We learn to serve selflessly and walk humbly. We learn to accept suffering, hardships, and trials with joy.

Jesus said:

"If you were of the world, the world would love you as its own; but because you are not of the world, but I chose you out of the world, therefore the world hates you. Remember the word that I said to you: 'A servant is not greater than his master.' If they persecuted me, they will also persecute you. If they kept my word, they will also keep yours." (John 15:19-20)

We would be foolish to think that Jesus was persecuted and hated by the world, but that we won't be. And yet, so many self-professing Christians do everything that they can to avoid any possibility of any form of persecution. Many of the people who fill the churches in this country keep their faith as private as they possibly can, because they fear the consequences of being disliked or maybe made fun of by their peers.

We need to understand how incredibly silly this seems in comparison to men and women in places around the world where violent persecution of Christians is commonplace. While we're crying "persecution!" every time someone mocks us or stands against us for expressing our faith, there's a man in Indonesia who watches as his family members are shot through the head, one by one, as each of them refuses to deny Christ. And when the persecutors finally come to the man, insisting that he deny Christ, he cries out, "Kill me if you must, but there is nothing that you can offer me that is worth denying Christ!" And if you don't think that this is a reality in numerous places around the world, you have not done your research, and you live in a very sheltered reality.

You cannot follow Jesus without being hated and/or persecuted one way or another—whether that means being threatened with death or mocked by your peers. Our attitude when it comes to persecution should be to rejoice rather than retreat, because persecution is a badge of faithfulness. That's why Peter said, "But rejoice insofar as you share Christ's sufferings, that you may also rejoice and be glad when his glory is revealed" (1st Peter 4:13).

For the person who lives for Jesus, there is gain in life—that is, there will be fruitful labor for Jesus, adding prolonged meaning and purpose to a person's life—and there is death in gain. What is the gain in death?

"I am hard pressed between the two. My desire is to depart and be with Christ, for that is far better." (Philippians 1:23)

He's hard-pressed between knowing whether it would be more profitable to live or to die. If he lives, he will continue to produce fruit from his labor. That's a good thing. But if he dies, he will be with Christ, which is also a good thing. In fact, he says that to depart and be with Christ is FAR better.

Do you feel the sense of certainty and assurance in Paul's words? Paul was a man who knew where he stood with God, and he eagerly anticipated the day when he would hear the Lord Jesus say to him, "Well done, good and faithful servant." The last words that Paul had heard from Jesus were spoken as Paul was on the road to Damascus, as he was the one persecuting Christians. I can only imagine that Paul couldn't wait to hear those words of approval from Jesus. And so he did not fear death. And because he was willing to die for his faith, he was free to live for it.

When a person is so afraid of death that they're afraid to live out their faith to the fullest, the truth is that they have become a slave to their own mortality.

What's your greatest hope? Is it something in this life? Because if it's something in this life, then to die is great loss, because the things of this world are not coming with us when we die.

For Paul, his greatest hope was not only to be like Christ, but also to be with Christ, in His presence, and so to die was gain, not because it meant the end of earthly suffering, but because to die meant that he could dwell in the direct presence of Christ, free to experience eternal fellowship with Him.

But there's another way that death is gain. If our goal is to glorify Christ in all that we do, dying can be a very powerful witness to Christ. If Paul died in a way that glorified Christ, then there was an additional gain in dying. It's been said that the blood of martyrs is the seed of the church, and indeed, if you look back through history, you'll find that when Christians are being martyred, the church doesn't just die out—instead, it prompts periods of great revival, because it separates the chaff from the wheat! And Paul is willing to be a martyr—he's willing to give his life for Jesus—because he's confident that it will bring glory to Christ in some way.

It is beautiful and wonderful to know that this very passage has actually been an encouragement to those who were about to be martyred.

Have you ever said to yourself, "Oh Lord, just take me home now!"? It's easy for us to leave that impression for people—as if we're just living for the icing on the cake (which is what heaven is). See, the reason that Paul is torn between these two options is that he's committed to the mission of God on earth, which is "to seek and save the lost" (Luke 19:10). And while we can probably all say that we would agree with Paul that it would be better to be with Jesus, can you honestly say that you'd be torn between living and dying (if you had any say in the matter), because you're so committed to what God has called you to do?

A few years ago, I set out to get in shape to run a half-marathon, and what I found out is that with long-distance running, you have to be focused on the finish line, yes, but it's important to focus on what's immediately in front of you—that is, to focus on what you have to do to get to the finish line. As anyone who has run long distance will tell you, the finish line for a 5K isn't as sweet as the finish line of a half marathon. And I am sure that the finish line of a half marathon is nowhere as sweet as the finish line of a full marathon. In other words, the longer and more difficult the race, the greater the sense of achievement and reward at the end. That's why Paul said, "For I consider that the sufferings of this present time are not worthy to be compared with the glory that is to be revealed to us" (Romans 8:18). That's why he said, "For momentary, light affliction is producing for us an eternal weight of glory far beyond all comparison" (2nd Corinthians 4:17). Do you see the correlation between affliction and the reward of entering into His glory?

We must guard ourselves against the temptation to be so eager to get to the finish line that we don't run the race with persistence and a steadfast mind. We have to guard against the temptation to be so homesick for heaven that we fail to participate in what God has called us to do now. And I just love that Paul is so committed to running the race well and fulfilling the mission that God had called him to that he finds both to be enticing.

We can become so focused on heaven that we forget the mission on earth, but we can also become so focused on the mission and doing God's work that we lose sight of heaven. This world is not our home—we're just passing through. The Bible describes us as "aliens" and "exiles" who live, work, and function upon the earth for a season, all the while "seeking a homeland" in heaven (Hebrews 11:1-14).

Paul isn't denying that he wants to cross the finish line. He does. But he is also enticed by the possibility of continuing his ministry, specifically to the Philippians. So he writes:

"But to remain in the flesh is more necessary on your account." (Philippians 1:24)

While Paul looked forward to heaven as much as anyone, he brings his personal desires into submission to the will of Christ with joyful acceptance. This church in Philippi still had problems—problems that Paul knew he could help them overcome and grow through. And maybe he was the best man for the job. He started the Christian movement in their city, and knew many of their leaders personally. Who would be better for the job?

What Paul is telling us here is that he was more than willing to place the NEEDS of others before his own personal desires. Do you realize how much conflict between Christians would be eliminated if we all followed Paul's example? We would eradicate splits and divisions within the church!

It's as if Paul is wanting so badly to cross the finish line, but he knows that there are some fellow runners in the race who are injured on the side of the road, and so he wants to tend to their needs and wounds before moving on to the finish line.

Once again, Paul is teaching us by example. This is what it looks like to take on the likeness of Christ and commit to a life of dedication to the selfless sacrificial service of our brothers and sisters in Christ. Part of running the race well means being willing to humble ourselves, forego our personal ambitions, and meet the needs within the body of Christ. This is one of the things that was so beautiful about the early church, and it's honestly something that is lacking in a world that is increasingly busy today.

There was a study done by Stanford University which revealed that there was a strong correlation between finding meaning in life and experiencing joy and happiness in life. According to this study, "People leading meaningful lives get a lot of joy from giving to others" (http://faculty-gsb.stanford.edu/aaker/pages/documents/SomeKeyDifferencesHappyLifeMeaningfulLife_2012.pdf). Likewise, the person who lives for Jesus must learn to give themselves to others.

The question is, what makes life meaningful? As Solomon observed, true meaning is only found in fearing and obeying God (Ecclesiastes 12:13). That means serving God, which entails the selfless, sacrificial serving of God's people. And when we do that, we too will be able to truly say, "To live is Christ, and to die is gain," because we joyfully bring our personal will into submission to the will of God, in order that, whether we live or die, He alone is glorified.

~~~

Chapter 5: The Joy of Christian Unity

Philippians 1:25-30

Every year on Super Bowl Sunday, the two best teams in the NFL compete on North America's biggest sports stage for the right to call themselves champions. There are no short-cuts to this game; even some of the league's best players never get the opportunity to play in the big game. In order to make it to the Super Bowl, your team has to beat out all of the other teams that are trying to bite and claw their way to the top.

The best chance that any team has to win a championship is to have flawless execution from all eleven men on the field during any given play. Without question, the more in sync with one another a team plays, the greater their chances of winning are going to be. But conversely, the less in sync a team plays together, the less their chances of winning are going to be.

One of the great things about football is the amount of involvement that each player on the field has in each play. See, in baseball, if you're playing left field, you could technically go a whole game without ever having to touch a baseball, and your team could win in a landslide. In basketball, you could do nothing but run wind-sprints all game, and your team could theoretically still win. But in football, every single player on the field has a job to do on every single play. There is no other major league, professional sport which requires that a team work together as tightly as football requires.

Imagine, for a moment, that you had one player who absolutely refused to do his job. For the sake of the illustration, let's imagine that you've got a wide receiver who only runs the routes that he thinks are best—he never runs the route that the quarterback is expecting him to run. In fact, rather than listening to the quarterback when he calls a play, he does his own play-calling for the team. Let's extend the illustration, and imagine that all of your wide receivers did the same thing, and so did your running back. If you understand football at all, you know that it would be impossible for such a team to make it to the Super Bowl. The odds of them ever winning a game would be slim to none.

What would ever give us the slightest idea that church is all that different? I suspect that if the game of football had been around in Paul's day, he may have used it as an illustration for the way that the church was intended to function. Paul used the body as an illustration, which is probably a better illustration anyway, since everyone knows how a body works, but not everyone knows how football is played. But you can't miss the fact that a football team works in a way that is similar to how the body works: each part has a different function and different abilities that fit with that function.

Why, then, does this conflict, in which one or more people aren't in sync with everyone else, exist within the church? It certainly existed in the Philippian church. Using the illustration of the body, why does it seem like the body of Christ has two left feet sometimes? Assuming that it's not a case of wheat and tares, it's ultimately because God isn't done with us yet; that's why. In the meantime, the desires of the flesh get in the way. But Paul has told the Philippians that he is confident that God will complete the work that He started in them . . . not because of how well they are functioning as a team or as a body, but in spite of how poorly they function together at times.

While Paul is sure of the fact that God will complete what He has begun in the Philippian Christians, he's also made it clear that he's not sure about something: whether he's going to live or die. He's waiting to stand trial before Nero as he writes this, and while he's unsure as to whether or not he'll live or die, he's sure that either way, Christ will be glorified, because for Paul, to live is Christ and to die is gain! And as he thinks about which seems more likely— that the Lord would allow him to remain alive and bearing fruit in his ministry or whether the Lord would take him home—he realizes, in verse 24, "But to remain in the flesh is more necessary on your account."

And so he continues, writing:

"Convinced of this, I know that I will remain and continue with you all, for your progress and joy in the faith, so that in me you may have ample cause to glory in Christ Jesus, because of my coming to you again." (Philippians 1:25-26)

There is no doubt about it, the Philippian church could benefit from having someone like Paul to stand with them and to help them to be purged of the strife and divisions that they were facing from within. And it's almost like the more Paul thinks about this, the more probable he feels it is that the Lord has more work for him to do here on earth.

There are two reasons that the Philippians needed someone like Paul. First, Paul realized that they needed him for the sake of progress in the faith. This obviously means a lot of things: it means understanding doctrine, but it also means growing in Christlikeness. There are few things that help us to grow in Christlikeness than to have someone who's a little further along on that journey than we are to stand beside us and coach us through the ups and downs of life. The last two times I've visited my parents in Las Vegas, I had the privilege of having lunch with Pastor Greg Massanari, who is my parents' pastor. He's one of the godliest and wisest men I have ever met, and he's able to strengthen me and help me grow because he's had so many years in ministry, he can relate to most of the challenges and feelings of inadequacy that pastors feel, and so he's able to sort of encourage and help coach me through them based on his experience.

That's the kind of role that Paul played for the church in Philippi. He could help them grow in the faith and navigate through some of the difficulties they were facing. And by doing that, he'd bring them to the second reason he was convinced that he would be more likely to continue in his earthly ministry: because the more progress a person has in the faith, the more joy they have in their faith. As one commentator noted, "Progress without joy is spurious; joy without progress is counterfeit." (Hansen)

If you wanted to use the analogy of the football team, Paul isn't the owner of the team (that would be Jesus, of course), but he's sort of like the coach. A coach needs to have an emotional connection to his players—an ability to relate to them and bring the best out in them. And there is joy in making strides toward being the best that a player can be.

And ultimately, Paul knew that if he would be able to remain alive and able to come and visit the Philippians, they would glory in Christ Jesus. Why? Because they would recognize it for what it is: an answer to their prayers. When we see God answer our prayers, it makes us excited to be a Christian, doesn't it? Have you ever had a prayer answered, and your response was something like, "Oh thank you, Lord Jesus! Thank You, thank You, thank You!" I remember the first day that my back stopped constantly hurting, just for a moment—long enough for me to walk a 10 minute walk to our car without needing to stop in order to keel over in pain. And I remember getting to the car and having my eyes well up with tears—not tears of pain, but of joy. I didn't know if my back was going to be hurting again five minutes later, but I was so thankful for those first ten minutes of having no pain, I think it's safe to say that I experienced what it was like in that moment to glory in Christ as a result of an answer to persistent prayer.

Those types of moments are important for our growth in Christ individually, but they're even more important as a collective group, because it brings a divided community to the point that people are more willing to let bygones be bygones, and people drop their grudges and celebrate together. This is what Paul has in mind.

While Paul was pretty confident that he would remain alive, however, he wasn't absolutely positive that that's what the outcome would be. For that reason, he sort of takes a step back to add a disclaimer, just in case everything goes wrong and Paul is unable to visit them, writing:

"Only let your manner of life be worthy of the gospel of Christ, so that whether I come and see you or am absent, I may hear of you that you are standing firm in one spirit, with one mind striving side by side for the faith of the gospel," (Philippians 1:27)

Here, Paul turns his attention to the primary reason for this letter: the strife and divisions that had risen up in the church in Philippi. We will learn in chapter 4 that it was a rivalry between two women—Euodia and Syntyche— although we don't actually know what the rivalry was about. I believe that that is for our benefit, because it would be horrible if the modern church said, "Well, this doesn't apply to us at all, because our rivalry is different." No, any and all rivalries within the church body need to be dealt with, not with one of the people just deciding to leave the church, but with both people taking ownership of their part in it and forgiving the other party or parties against whom they've held feelings of discord or disharmony.

Sadly, this is one of those issues that we take far too lightly, but upon which the Scriptures give an incredible amount of emphasis. God's word tells us that apart from coming to Christ, there's not a whole lot in life that takes priority over living in harmony and unity with our fellow Christians. We're like a family, and family life is messy. You have siblings that bicker over ridiculous things. You have the nutty aunt that you always feel like you need to apologize in advance for. You have the uncle whom you wish you could just keep tucked away in a closet somewhere. But despite all of this, the family loves each other and sticks together. And that takes work.

So what options do people have when there is an interpersonal conflict in the church? Well, first of all, they can leave. There is no Biblical precedent for this at all. The Bible is all about reconciliation and harmony. First, we are to be reconciled to God in order that we may have peace with Him, and then we are to remain constantly reconciled to others in order to have peace with them. Paul addresses interpersonal conflicts a few times in his letters, and never once does he encourage someone to jump ship and find another church body to be a part of. Instead, what he told the Romans, for example was "so far as it depends on you, live peaceably with all" (Romans 12:18). That does not mean running away. It means working through it together.

See, when a person just decides to leave without working it out, they're cheating themselves out of a chance to see God's glory as it's only revealed in reconciliation. You miss the increased closeness in a relationship with the other person as well, which is also only done through reconciliation. And not only is the person who leaves cheating themselves, but they're cheating everyone else in the church body, because they won't be able to witness those things either. To leave is certainly not walking in a manner that is worthy of the Gospel, because the Gospel is about grace. As recipients of God's grace, we should be eager to demonstrate grace to one another, and leaving prevents that from happening.

The second option is to stay, but not address the issues. This has a lot of the same problems as leaving. Holding resentment and/or bitterness against someone is ultimately cheating and poisoning yourself. I've often said that holding onto bitterness is like drinking poison and expecting the person you're bitter toward to die. Because we hate conflict, this is the road that people usually try to choose—and I am no exception. But what I've found—not only in my own experience, but also in what I've seen in the lives of others—is that holding onto unforgiveness or anger doesn't resolve it. Instead, it creates increasing distance from the person you're angry with, while leaving that person wondering why there is an increased distance. And again, I'm preaching to myself as much as I'm preaching to anyone else here. Refusing to deal with an offense isn't even a real option—it's just postponing until you're ready to explode, while suffocating the relationship until you get to that point.

The third option is to walk in a manner worthy of the Gospel. What does that mean? It means reconciling and demonstrating grace toward our brothers and sisters in Christ. We can know that much just by taking a guess at what Paul means. But we don't have to guess, because while Paul doesn't expound a whole lot on what it means to walk in a manner worthy of the Gospel here, he does expound on it elsewhere.

"Walk in a manner worthy of the Lord, fully pleasing to him, bearing fruit in every good work and increasing in the knowledge of God. May you be strengthened with all power, according to his glorious might, for all endurance and patience with joy, giving thanks to the Father, who has qualified you to share in the inheritance of the saints in light." (Colossians 1:10-12)

Here, Paul defines what he means when he talks about walking in a manner that is worthy of the Lord and of His glorious Gospel. It means pleasing God in every way. How? In two ways: by bearing fruit (fruit of the Spirit) and increasing in the knowledge of God. Quick question: how do we bear fruit, according to John 15:4-5? By abiding in Jesus!

Walking in a manner worthy of the Gospel also involves seeking our strength in the glorious might of the Lord. Why do we need His power? For all endurance and patience and joy. Do you think you might need endurance and patience when you're dealing with groups of people with different personalities? You'd better believe it!

Walking in a manner worthy of the Gospel means giving thanks to the Father for qualifying you to share in the inheritance of the saints. You didn't qualify yourself for this inheritance of eternal life and fellowship with God. He qualified you. That levels the playing field between fellow believers, doesn't it? Because none of us deserves it more than anyone else. It's all God's grace.

Walking in a manner worthy of the Gospel means walking differently than the world walks. The world is built on social hierarchies. Human nature dictates that when we're enemies with someone, we desire some type of harm to them, whether that means physically hurting them or hurting them by avoiding them and keeping our distance. But God calls us to love our enemies. He didn't call us to do something that He Himself didn't do, however, because we were all enemies of God by nature, and yet He loved us. How dare we not extend the same grace to others-- especially the people whom Jesus redeemed on the cross? God's Kingdom is built on grace and humility—it's built on love, joy, peace, patience, kindness, goodness, faithfulness, gentleness, and self-control. Because this is better than what the world has to offer in every way!

What we need to understand here, first and foremost, is that walking in a manner worthy of the gospel is bigger and better than anything that anyone could possibly strive for on a personal level. You want to hold a grudge against someone? Walking in a manner worthy of the Gospel is better. You want to exalt your power over leaders in your church? Walking in a manner worthy of the Gospel is better. You want to fit your own agenda into the agenda of the church? Walking in a manner worthy of the Gospel is better.

So what do you do when you come across someone in the church whose personality feels to you like sandpaper, and you're a block of soft wood? You walk in a manner that is worthy of the Gospel—you forgive, and when you're offended by them, you deal with them privately in accordance with what Jesus instructed in Matthew 5:23-24 when He said, "if you are offering your gift at the altar and there remember that your brother has something against you, leave your gift there before the altar and go. First be reconciled to your brother, and then come and offer your gift."

So Paul thinks that it's probably more likely that he'll remain alive and be able to come and see the church in Philippi, but he's not sure. So he says "whether I come and see you or am absent, I may hear of you that you are standing firm in one spirit, with one mind striving side by side for the faith of the gospel."

In one way or another, Paul kept tabs on the churches in the region. To the Romans, he wrote that "your faith is being reported all over the world" (Romans 1:8). To the church in Corinth, he expressed some disgust at their reputation, writing, "It is actually reported that there is sexual immorality among you" (1st Cor. 5:1). To the church in Galatia, he expressed even more disgust, writing, "I am astonished that you are so quickly deserting Him who called you in the grace of Christ and are turning to a different gospel" (Galatians 1:6). In one way or another, Paul found out about what the churches he was affiliated with were going through. And so even if he wasn't able to physically visit the Philippian church, he would inevitably receive word about their progression . . . or their regression. He'd hear about progression if the people chose to walk in a manner worthy of the Gospel. He'd hear of regression if they didn't.

Paul gives us two keys to the kind of progress he's hoping to hear about. First, they must stand firm in one spirit. This is so hard for us in our culture, because we're such a consumerist culture—if we don't like the service we get at one restaurant, there are ten others that would love to have our business. If you order a computer, you customize it so that you get exactly what you want. And so what happens within the church is that we develop this mindset that it's all about us, and we should be doing things the way we want to do things and the way we like to do things, because the customer is king! This leads us AWAY from walking in a manner worthy of the Gospel, because it encourages us NOT to stand firm in one spirit.

The hostility that we face from the enemy of God and from the world is designed to destroy us by dividing us. But Jesus, on the night that He was handed over to the Roman authorities, prayed for His followers and for the followers of His followers. In other words, He prayed for us, saying, "Holy Father, keep them in your name, which you have given Me, that they may be one, even as We are one" (John 17:11). This matters to Jesus! It's really, really important to Him. If we desire to be obedient to Him, we must have enough resolve that we refuse to compromise or back down on this one, and we find the power and strength to do that through the Spirit—the Holy Spirit. The Spirit of God unites us, bonds us together, and strengthens us to stand together, overcoming anything that would seek to divide us, because the truth is that we're better together than we are divided.

Secondly, we must work—strive—side by side, with one mind. The Greek word for "strive" is used to describe a military unit, as the soldiers of the unit stand by one another to advance against the enemy. The picture that

Paul is giving us is of a group that is so united together, they're not seen as striving individually but all together as one person. Using the football analogy, everyone clearly understands and is committed to carrying out the play that gets called. And so they're advancing the football down the field, because they're all of one mind. You don't advance the ball by striving AGAINST one another; you do it by striving WITH one another.

And Paul instructs them to do these two things in order to advance the faith of the gospel. To spread the good news of forgiveness that each person so desperately needs to hear. And when we work with one another rather than against one another, we have less and less reason to fear the opposition.

"and not frightened in anything by your opponents."
(Philippians 1:28a)

From the perspective of the flesh, there was much to be fearful of and intimidated by for the Philippian Christians. You remember how Paul was thrown into a jail cell for spreading the Gospel in their city. It was a hostile environment. And Paul knew that if he was persecuted for his faithfulness in sharing the Gospel message, those who lived in the city could expect more of the same themselves.

Who were their opponents? The Roman Empire—that was a big one. But don't overlook the same pagans who had Paul and Silas thrown in jail, not to mention any false teachers who might sneak into their midst. Think about it: how easy would it have been for someone to come in and say, "God is obviously punishing Paul, and thus what Paul taught you isn't true!" This is one of the central doctrines of the prosperity gospel, which is no gospel at all, which teaches that the more faith you have, the more God will bless you. Therefore, you'll be healthy and wealthy. This is a concept that is completely foreign to the Bible, but it's so enticing to our flesh! Unlike health and wealth, suffering and persecution have a cleansing effect on God's people. J.C. Ryle once said, "Trials are intended to make us think, to wean us from the world, to send us to the Bible, and to drive us to our knees." It lifts our eyes away from worldly distractions, it strengthens our desire to be in God's presence and forces us to remember that this world is not our home, it serves as an example for others to follow and gives us empathy and a heart to minister to others who suffer. And it destroys the weed that never took root—in other words, it chases false converts away.

Paul makes it clear that a church that is standing together in the unity that God created them to experience, they won't be frightened or intimidated. But this type of unity is also solid evidence of something:

"This is a clear sign to them of their destruction, but of your salvation, and that from God." (Philippians 1:28b)

The Christians in Philippi would be persecuted, but if they would stand together to advance the Gospel, their unity would be a clear sign of the impending doom of their persecutors. Why? Because it's not natural for people to stick together through difficult circumstances. Do you see the irony here? Their opponents—those who persecuted them—sought their destruction, but by doing so, they were receiving a sign of their own destruction.

But their unity in the face of persecution would also serve as evidence of the salvation of those in the church. The same holds true for us. If we're facing trials and stick together anyway, it's evidence of the fact that we are indeed saved. We must stand together expecting to face trials and suffering. Suffering for the sake of the Gospel is not a curse—it's an honor. That's why Paul finishes up this section, writing:

"For it has been granted to you that for the sake of Christ you should not only believe in Him but also suffer for His sake, engaged in the same conflict that you saw I had and now hear that I still have." (Philippians 1:29-30)

You might find it shocking to learn that this word "granted" is derived from the same Greek root word that means "grace." It's hard to see persecution and suffering as a form of grace, isn't it? It is . . . until you've been through the ringer a few times. I haven't ever grown as much in my faith as I did during the three and a half months last summer that my back was constantly in pain. That wasn't persecution, but it was certainly suffering. There's grace in our suffering because it causes our growth—sometimes it even causes exponential growth.

Paul wanted to make sure that the Philippians knew, without any question, that suffering and persecution weren't a form of punishment from God. It wasn't something that happened outside of God's will. No, it was perfectly in accordance with God's will, and it was proof of the fact that they belonged to Jesus. Of course, Jesus told His disciples that if they world hated and persecuted Him, the church could expect the same thing for themselves.

As Christians, and as a church, we're all in the same boat, and we're in this together. We're a family. Sometimes we're a dysfunctional family, but we stick together, because that's our calling—that's what a family does. Not one of us stands alone, and let us never dare to isolate, separate, or divide ourselves from the group, because God's desire is that we stand together, because we're better together than we are apart. As Jesus said in John 13:34-35, "A new commandment I give to you, that you love one another: just as I have loved you, you also are to love one another. By this all people will know that you are my disciples, if you have love for one another." The joy of Christian unity is found both in the message it sends to the world and in the assurance it gives us that we belong to Jesus.

~~~

Chapter 6: Grow Up or Blow Up

Philippians 2:1-4

As I write this, the Seattle Seahawks—my current hometown team—just won the 2014 Super Bowl. It's not the first time I've lived in a city that won a national championship—I actually lived in Las Vegas when the UNLV Runnin' Rebels won the NCAA Basketball National Championship in 1990. I lived in Dallas when the Cowboys won the Super Bowl in 1996. I lived in Denver when the Broncos won the Super Bowl in 1998. You would think that sports cities would be paying me just to live there, right? Well, I can honestly say that I've never seen anything like I've seen over the course of the past week. Seattle absolutely has the most insane sports fans I've ever seen in my life, and it was all out on full public display this past week after the Seahawks won.

Of course, one of the things that teams do when they win a national championship is have a parade. I've can honestly say that I've never seen anything like what we saw for the Seahawks' parade! It never got above freezing temperatures that day, but people camped out overnight just to be able to see it, and we surely all saw pictures from the parade. It was insane. In a city with a population of roughly 635,000 they had a turnout of 750,000! And when you have that many people, do you know what else you have? You have a lot of garbage. On the night after the parade, the local news was interviewing the people who had to clean up the streets after the parade. In their first run through, they collected over one ton of garbage—a whole ton of paper and plastic bottles that people just thoughtlessly tossed on the city streets, and they weren't even done yet. And that's not the shocking part. The shocking part, for me, was the attitude of the guys cleaning it up. They were ecstatic! They were so psyched to be cleaning up. One of the guys they interviewed said that it was one of the greatest honors of his life.

If you're like me, that hits you hard. You might be asking, why were these guys so happy to be cleaning up other peoples' garbage? Because, as one of the street cleaners said, without them, there could be no parade, and they were so happy that their Seahawks won, they counted it a privilege to clean up the mess. Hey, not everyone gets that responsibility, right?

The reality that smacks us upside the head here is that we're supposed to have that same attitude toward our brothers and sisters in Christ. Now, I'm just going to warn you in advance that the second chapter of Philippians is one of those chapters that stretches us and challenges us—maybe it even lays the smack down on you, so to speak. The reason that this is such a tough chapter is because it's taking aim right at a weakness that every single one of us struggles with: pride. And pride is one of those things about which we can say, the bigger it is, the harder it falls. With each verse in this chapter, Paul is chopping away, and if you internalize what he has to say, your pride won't stand for long. And that can be painful--good, undoubtedly, but painful.

You see, there's a huge thing in each of us that loves to be served; it's called the ego. The ego is this carnal, worldly thing that we're born with that rules our hearts from the day that we're born. And because of this ego thing, every one of us wants to just throw our proverbial trash on the street and let someone else clean it up. It doesn't want to be a person in attendance at the parade, and it certainly doesn't want to clean up after the parade—it wants to be the center of attention in the parade, which, of course, the world views as pretty much the polar opposite of being the one to clean it all up. But God doesn't call us to be the center of attention in the proverbial parade—that's a role that belongs to Jesus. What He does call us to do is to serve. Because if nobody serves, there's no parade.

But this is exactly how Jesus demanded that things would work in His kingdom. He said that in His kingdom, "the last will be first, and the first last" (Matthew 20:16). And then He showed His disciples what He meant by washing the feet of the disciples—the nasty, smelly, dirty, calloused, maybe fungally-infected feet of twelve grown men. And you thought that the idea of cleaning up paper and plastic bottles on the street sounded bad. But think about who's doing this—that's the job of a servant, but Jesus says, "I have given you an example, that you also should do just as I have done to you" (John 13:15).

Just in case we miss the point of all of this, I want to make sure that we understand that Jesus wasn't saying we should just wash one another's feet. No, He's essentially saying, "Serve one another, and be eager to serve."

This type of thinking is totally contrary to everything we grow up thinking and believing about ourselves. But Jesus says, "A servant is not greater than his Master" (John 13:16). Who's the Master? Jesus is. Who's the servant? You and me—the people Jesus gave His life to redeem.

Now, if you think that this type of thinking is difficult because it's just so contrary to carnal human nature, how much more difficult is it for us to act this way toward people with whom we have some type of conflict or division? The church is supposed to represent the only One who brings true peace—and yet, so often, we are marked by internal conflict. That's the situation in the church in Philippi, and that's the reason that Paul lays out one of the most challenging chapters in all of Scripture.

"So if there is any encouragement in Christ, any comfort from love, any participation in the Spirit, any affection and sympathy, complete my joy by being of the same mind, having the same love, being in full accord and of one mind." (Philippians 2:1-2)

Now, the first question that comes to mind when I read this is, "What does Paul mean by 'if there is any encouragement in Christ?'" The word for encouragement means "to help," and it's derived from the word *paraklete*, which is the name by which Jesus referred to the Holy Spirit when He said that He would ask the Father, and the Father would send a Helper (John 14:26, 15:26). So Paul is saying that if there is any help to be found by being in Christ—that is, if He makes any difference at all in your life and if the Holy Spirit is actively participating in your life—then you have the power to resolve your differences with one another. And friends, please don't ever forget that the power of Christ is within His people to forgive every offense against us and be reconciled with the offending person. If we are in Christ, this is a resource in Him that we must learn to continually tap into.

Don't get me wrong here: for the person who is in Christ, there is no "if" about it. But Paul poses it as a question in order to challenge these Christians to examine themselves and find that the power to resolve conflict is within them because the power of the Holy Spirit is within them.

Listen, it is not difficult to find flaws in other people, and there is a temptation for us to focus on those flaws, especially if our ego already feels threatened in some way by someone else. And what do we do when we're in that situation? We focus on that person's flaws, and we want to make sure that everyone else sees those flaws as clearly as we do. When we do that, what we're really doing is seeking some sort of approval from others and some kind of justification within our own minds of not honoring or respecting or submitting ourselves to that other person—or, worse yet, separating ourselves completely from them. And the way we approach it is to treat the whole situation in a way that says, "I've got no other choice!"

But Paul is telling us that that is a lie—we do have a choice! We don't have to focus on the flaws of a fellow brother or sister in Christ. We absolutely CAN resolve any and every conflict we might have with another believer. Because every difference we have with other Christians is reconcilable when we learn to live with the mind and the humility of Jesus. One of the secrets is to quit focusing on the flaws and failures of the other person and focus on what you have in common with one another: an eternal inheritance together in Christ.

Now, I had a long and drawn out discussion just a few weeks ago with a fellow brother in Christ who was upset that I criticized a well-known preacher who not only denies the doctrine of the Trinity, but also affirms and preaches the prosperity gospel. This is a preacher who is NOT a brother in Christ—in fact, he's affiliated with the Oneness Pentecostal cult and believes all sorts of nutty things about God's nature and His relationship to humanity (as does everyone who teaches the prosperity gospel). And my friend was telling me that I should just put any differences I have with this false teacher aside in the name of Christian unity.

Scripture has much to say about distancing ourselves from and handling someone who preaches a false gospel and denies any central, defining doctrine of Christianity (which the doctrine of the Trinity is). Galatians 1:9 comes to mind. But for the brother or sister who is in Christ who isn't committing some type of heresy or affirming a false gospel, we must look past our differences and remain reconciled and at peace with them, because the comfort of Christ's love should unite Christians with one another to the point where we feel affection and sympathy toward any and every fellow brother and sister in Christ. What we share in common with other Christians is greater than the sum of every offense.

And Paul is saying, "If this is a reality in your life to even the slightest degree, then . . ." what? Then Paul's joy will be complete because they'll be of one mind—in other words, they'll be like-minded, working toward a common goal with the same game plan. We've filled our quota of football illustrations, but let's look at it now like a symphony. There is nothing that's more confusing when you're playing an instrument than being on the wrong page or playing the wrong note. The musician hears the other instruments, and realizes immediately when his own instrument isn't playing the same thing as the other instruments. What do you get when everyone has been told to play a beautiful piece together, and yet they're all playing something different? You get chaos—it's called a cacophony. Or, if you're playing electric instruments, maybe they call it experimental punk or something. Whatever you call it, lack of harmony in music produces something that is nowhere near as beautiful as what was intended.

But here's what happens in the mind of the musician when that happens: the musician starts trying to figure out WHY it's happening. Is it because so-and-so is on the wrong song? And what ends up happening when we're not on the same page with others relationally, and therefore not living in peace with the offending party, is we start coming up with all sorts of excuses and reasons to justify our own actions. It's as if the thought never enters our minds that WE might be the ones in the wrong. That's a dangerous place to be.

Reconciling with one another starts with being on the same page—being like-minded with one another. As Christians, we have that. We've all been called to the same mission. That mission supersedes our differences on a personal level. That's what will lead to Paul's joy being full.

The key to this, Paul says, is to remember that we have the same love. We all love Jesus, and He loves us. And so if we're going to strive to be like Christ, we must strive not only to love Him, but to love His church the way that He does. Once we realize that we have a common commitment to love as Christ loves, the offenses that have hurt us will be much easier to recover from and forgive. A commitment to Christ-like love is the glue that will bond a divided community back together.

Paul says that this is what it will take to make his joy complete. That phrase should ring a bell, right? We remember that Jesus said this:

"If you keep My commandments, you will abide in My love, just as I have kept My Father's commandments and abide in His love. These things I have spoken to you, that

88

my joy may be in you, and that your joy may be full."
(John 15:10-11)

And this is the same night that Jesus said, "A new
command I give to you: that you love one another." See,
our tendency is to think that if we hold bitterness against
some fellow Christian, it doesn't affect anyone else, but
that just isn't true. Paul is saying that his joy isn't complete,
not because anything is lacking on his end, but because of
what is lacking amongst the Philippians: unity.

Have you ever injured part of your body? Obviously, I
have—I think we all have, in one way or another. And what
happens when you injure one part of your body is that the
other parts of your body work to compensate for your
injury. So an injury to one part of the body can affect the
whole body, and Paul is saying that the same is true of the
church—when one part isn't functioning correctly, the
whole thing isn't functioning properly. Nobody's joy is full
or complete because there's unresolved strife in their midst.
So what are you waiting for? Resolve any and all strife
immediately!

And here's what ties all of this together. Look at verse 5.
Paul tells us that the power to do all of these things is
within our grasp.

*"Have this mind among yourselves, which is yours in
Christ Jesus." (Philippians 2:5)*

What mind should we have amongst ourselves? One that is
dedicated to living out the Gospel, which means living in a
manner that is selfless and humble. It means having our
priorities lined up correctly. It means being committed to
doing our part in being rightly related, both to God and to
His people. It means walking in a manner that is worthy of

our calling by working it out when conflict arises. Keep this verse in mind, because, as I said, this is really what ties all of this together. It's what makes all of this possible. This mind is ours in Christ Jesus.

Paul will now give us instructions on doing that successfully and authentically.

"Do nothing from selfish ambition or conceit, but in humility count others more significant than yourselves. Let each of you look not only to his own interests, but also to the interests of others." (Philippians 2:3-4)

Look how this is structured: first Paul tells us what not to do, and then he tells us what to replace that behavior with. The first behavior or attitude to avoid is selfish ambition, which is similar to conceit, but they're not exactly the same thing. Conceit drives selfish ambition, and so Paul wants to make sure that we get the point: we've got to pull any proverbial weeds up by the root. We've seen this term "selfish ambition" before—Paul used it to describe those who were preaching the gospel not for the glory of Christ but for the glory of themselves, out of a sense of rivalry with Paul. Paul is essentially saying, "Don't be like them in the way that you act toward your fellow brothers and sisters in Christ."

Selfishness and conceit are the two ugliest, nastiest, most deplorable aspects of the flesh. Every one of us has or will have a struggle with them. It's what lies at the root of every sin we commit, and we can very easily get so preoccupied with other sins that it causes to spring up in our lives, we often fail to see the damage that it causes on a relational level.

What do selfish ambition and conceit do on a relational level? They cause you to think of yourself—your ambitions, your wants, your desires, your plans—and to give your wants priority over someone else's. You see this in marriages all the time, unfortunately. You have two people who are not committed to dealing with selfish ambition and conceit, and it is a time-bomb just waiting to explode! A marriage will not last under those conditions—something will have to give. But the same ultimately holds true in any type of relationship. And so we have two options to choose from: blow up or grow up.

Most people choose to just blow it up. In the context of marriage, they decide to divorce, or they sabotage the relationship with infidelity. In the context of church, they throw their hands up and decide to leave out of bitterness. In the context of a friendship, the wedge between the two just keeps driving them further and further apart, to the point where you don't call or talk—maybe you just exchange annual Christmas cards. This is where selfish ambition and conceit lead, every single time! This is how you blow it up: you just continue operating from the nastiest aspect of the flesh nature. And when we choose to operate in a self-serving manner with others, we can be sure that it will eventually blow up. You want to destroy unity in a church? This is the way to do it: you get a bunch of people together who aren't interested in humility, and who just want to have their way or no way. And you try to put them in a room together. It's not going to last. Something must give, or it will fall to pieces.

But you don't have to do that. The alternative to blowing up is growing up. How do we do that? Paul tells us—it's the opposite of operating out of selfish ambition and conceit—by considering others more significant than ourselves. I warned you that this chapter was going to lay the smack down on us! But this is the mark of a truly mature, "grown-up" Christian: they're able to consider other people more important than they themselves are. That's not even to necessarily say that the other person actually IS more important, but that's not what it's really all about. It's really all about choosing humility over prideful behavior, and choosing to be the least rather than the greatest because that's how things operate in God's kingdom. The antidote for selfishness is selflessness.

One of the things you'll find in a mature believer is an awareness of what a wretched sinner they are. Isn't that funny? Because the more a person grows in Christ, the less they sin. And yet the less a person sins, the more aware they are of their sin, and the more it hurts, and the more they come to realize that if it wasn't for God's grace sustaining their faith despite their personal weakness, they would fall away in two seconds. And this type of Christian, who realizes that they're totally wretched on their own, wouldn't dare to exalt himself or herself over others. The mature believer's standing before God keeps them humble—not just before God, but also with God's people. And this is Paul's advice: grow in things like patience and humility and love for one another, because that's sufficient to heal any relational divisions.

The second thing he tells us not to do is to look to our own interests. That's what our Bibles say, but in the original language, the word "interest" isn't there. It would say, "Let each of you look not only to his own, but also to that of others." That sentence doesn't make any sense in English, and so the translators inserted the word "interests." But it's more ambiguous than just that. Do you have needs? Look also to the needs of others. Do you have a preference? Look also to the preferences of others.

This is a parallel from the previous verse. When we look ONLY to our own interests, needs, preferences, or what have you, and we don't look any further than the tip of our own noses, we're back to operating out of selfish ambition and conceit. The Greek word that gets translated as "look" literally means "to take aim." The word is *skopeo*, which sounds remarkably similar to "scope," doesn't it? In other words, Paul is saying that we shouldn't make our own interests or needs the goals that we aim for. Oh, how many quarrels and divisions would be eliminated if we all took this to heart and thus had nobody among us aiming toward their own interests.

We have to learn to ask ourselves, "Is this all about me, or am I looking out for everyone else's interests and preferences in addition to my own?" Paul isn't saying that we should neglect our own needs, but to ALSO remain intentionally mindful of the needs of others in addition to our own. And so the challenge is not to surround yourself with people who are exactly like you, but to surround yourself with people who **aren't** like you, but with whom you share the common bond of being in Christ, and to learn to place their interests on par with your own.

Again, we have a choice to make: are we going to be self-absorbed, or are we going to see the spiritual interests and needs of others as being equally important to our own? Because the more we learn to do this, the less desire we'll have to act out of selfish ambition.

Of course, the perfect model for all of this is Jesus Christ Himself, who surrendered His personal comfort for the sake of taking on flesh, living a perfectly sinless life, and dying on Calvary in order to save anyone and everyone who would trust in Him alone for salvation. He is the ultimate model of selflessness, and the more we become like Him, the more selfless we too will become.

Ambition, conceit, pride, and self-centeredness: these are the types of things that spark disharmony among Christians, and they poison our fellowship and bond with one another. This requires a radical transformation in us, away from the values of the world and growth in the values of God. We can be certain that the enemy of God will seek to divide us, and thus we must remember that we're better together. So we must never stop growing, both in our love for Jesus and for each other, because teaching people to love and honor one another the way that God's word calls us to love and honor one another is something that only God can truly do in us. He makes reconciliation with other Christians available to us through Christ and through the power of the Holy Spirit when we commit ourselves to loving Him and loving others the way that He loves us. And when we choose to grow in these two ways, it sends a message to the world, and the Gospel advances because God's work in us is on display for the entire world to see.

~~~

Chapter 7: The Biblical Model for Conflict Resolution

Philippians 2:5-11

A website called "Business Insider" featured an article last year which was titled "7 Brutally Honest Job Rejection Letters." As I read through these, I couldn't help but become even more convinced of the depravity of humanity, as they are absolutely heartless (which I suppose makes them somewhat humorous, because it's hard to believe that anyone could be so ruthless), but it also reminded me of the fact that conflict is one of the universal elements of the human experience.

One of the featured letters is from Sub Pop Records, an independent label from the Seattle area. They write, "Dear Loser, Thank you for sending your demo materials to Sun Pop for consideration. Presently, your demo package is one of a massive quantity of material we receive every day at Sub Pop World Headquarters, and is on its way through the great lower intestines that is the talent acquisitions process. We appreciate your interest and wish the best in your pursuit. P.S. This letter is known as a 'rejection letter.'"

The New Delta Review, which is a literary magazine out of Baton Rouge, Louisiana, wrote this to someone who had submitted something: "Thank you for submitting. Unfortunately, the work you sent is quite terrible. Please forgive the form rejection, but it would take too much of my time to tell you exactly how terrible it was. So again, sorry for the form letter."

One would think that these responses were just looking to pick a fight. And we can easily laugh at these examples and dismiss them as ridiculous, but the truth is that conflict is a normal part of our relationships. We have established that every relationship will involve conflict, if given sufficient time. And so before we continue in our study on the book of Philippians, which is specifically written to address conflict in the church, there are some Biblical principles relating to conflict that I want us to understand.

Conflict Has Been a Part of Human Existence Since The Garden of Eden

The book of Genesis tells us that in the beginning, God created the heavens and the earth and everything contained therein, including humanity. It was all good. It was perfect. It was free from corruption. There was no conflict . . . but that didn't last long. Conflict entered into human existence with one simple question:

"Did God actually say, 'You shall not eat of any tree in the garden'?" (Genesis 3:1)

This was immediately followed by a lie: "You will not surely die. For God knows that when you eat of it your eyes will be opened, and you will be like God" (vv. 4b-5a).

Eve faced a temptation and a dilemma unlike she had ever experienced before. The temptation to be content with what she had or to exalt herself to become like God—or so she thought. The dilemma was between obedience to God or becoming equal to God, and her desire to be equal to God won out over her desire to obey Him. This was the

96

first instance of conflict in all of human existence, and it was completely within Eve.

And yet as soon as this internal conflict was finished, the second one began, as she gave the fruit to Adam as well. Suddenly, God called out to Adam, but Adam hid because he was naked and afraid. What was he afraid of? He was afraid because his fellowship—his communion . . . his relationship—with God was suddenly broken off. Suddenly, Adam and Eve realized that their disobedience provoked conflict with a holy God who cannot tolerate even the smallest of sins, as Adam tried to point the finger of blame at God and at Eve.

Of course, this was the fall of all of humanity. The potential for perfect righteousness, which had been in them when God created them, was suddenly gone. And because they no longer had the potential for perfect righteousness within themselves, their offspring could not have the potential for perfect righteousness either.

We learn shortly thereafter that Adam and Eve had children, including two sons, named Cain and Abel. And we know that Cain ended up murdering Abel out of jealousy. Again, there's this conflict. Humanity was immediately living in broken, conflict-filled relationships with one another. This is part of the curse of sin, and it will plague our existence until the promises and prophecies of Revelation 21 and 22 are fulfilled.

"No longer will there be anything accursed . . ."
(Revelation 22:3)

And here we are, living in between Genesis 3 and Revelation 22. During this time, all human relationships experience a penchant for brokenness, turmoil, and conflict.

As a result, we have things like selfish ambition, pride, disagreements, and differing desires and preferences which must be dealt with. The question is, can we deal with them in a way that doesn't involve sin? And the answer is yes, which brings us to our next point.

Conflict is Not Necessarily Sinful

Given that we will experience conflict in every context of human relationships, we need to understand that there is often a sinful component to conflict, but that there doesn't NEED to be a sinful component. Conflict doesn't have to involve sin, but if we insist on handling it our way instead of God's way, sin will be unavoidable. Conflict always involves some degree of anger, but anger is not necessarily sinful. As Paul wrote to the Ephesians,

"Be angry, and do not sin." (Ephesians 4:26)

The thing that we need to understand is that sinfulness in conflict is found in the way that we respond to our feelings of anger. After all, God is angry toward sin, and yet He Himself does not sin. So the answer isn't to dismiss angry feelings, it's to deal with those feelings in a righteous manner.

During the three years of His earthly ministry, Jesus Himself constantly faced conflict—and if He had to face conflict, what would ever lead us to believe that we won't face it if we act in a Christlike manner? In fact, the more we become like Christ, the more likely we are to experience conflict with non-Christians, because we have opposing (not just different) sets of values. Knowing what we do about the likes of Paul and Peter, we can only imagine how much conflict they stirred up, just because they were passionate about what they believed.

If we take a look at the 15th chapter of Acts, we will understand why some have referred to it as the "conflict chapter" of the New Testament. The chapter opens with some Judaizers coming in and teaching Gentiles that they must be circumcised in order to be saved. So what do we read in verse 2?

"And after Paul and Barnabas had no small dissension and debate with them . . ." (Acts 15:2)

This happened at the church in Antioch. The church's response was to send Paul and Barnabas and a few others down to Jerusalem to consult with the other apostles on the issue. Once they got to Jerusalem, they started sharing about the wonderful things that were happening among the Gentiles, and how there was reason to rejoice. But the good news is interrupted.

"But some believers who belonged to the party of the Pharisees rose up . . ." (Acts 15:5)

What's all of this conflict about? It's ultimately about preserving the purity of the Gospel. Sadly, we still have these types of conflict, but we need to know that there is a way to handle the conflict which honors God, and there's a way to handle conflict which doesn't honor God. In this case, the apostles hold a counsel with the elders to discuss the matter.

"And after there had been much debate . . ." (Acts 15:7)

Let me ask this question: who was involved in this conflict? It was Christians. All of the people involved here were people who loved the Lord and who desired to preserve the truth of the Gospel message. And yet, while there was much conflict, there was no sin. Why not? Because they were talking through the issues which were sparking the conflict. They weren't back-biting or gossiping or slandering one another. They sat down with one another and had an open discussion.

Paul and Barnabas return to the church in Antioch to report the verdict: that circumcision isn't necessary for the Gentiles. But look at what we find starting in verse 36.

"And after some days Paul said to Barnabas, 'Let us return and visit the brothers in every city where we proclaimed the word of the Lord, and see how they are.' Now Barnabas wanted to take with them John called Mark. But Paul thought best not to take with them one who had withdrawn from them in Pamphylia and had not gone with them to the work. And there arose a sharp disagreement, so that they separated from each other." (Acts 15:36-39)

What is missing in this picture? Where's the conversation? Where's the open dialogue? What about what Jesus said about going to your brother and seeking reconciliation? Where's the prayer about such a major decision? Do you see how ridiculous it is that all of these Christians maintained their unity and didn't sin against one another when it came to a major issue, but then when it comes to John-Mark coming to serve the Lord, there's a divide? And yet, if you look around, you'll see the same thing happening between fellow brothers and sisters in Christ over things that are more petty, arbitrary, and ridiculous than this.

The point of all of this is simply to say that conflict is normal, but that there is a way to handle conflict that doesn't involve sin, and there is a way to handle conflict that does involve sin. That brings us to our next principle of conflict.

Conflict Between Christians Can Have Positive Results

In fact, I would say that if the conflict is handled in the right way, it will almost always have positive results. We must remember that every single one of us is involved in a war against an enemy whose presence we cannot physically see, but whose presence is evident in the fact that conflict often arises over the pettiest of things. We aren't engaged in a war in which the body is attacked; we're in a war in which the mind, spirit, and emotions are the enemy's preferred targets. We're fragile and we're vulnerable, and the enemy will exploit that to his advantage, every opportunity he gets. The more mindful we become of this reality, the more determined we must be to unite based on what we have in common: the love of Jesus. When we're unhappy with a fellow brother or sister in Christ, we must resolve to work out the things that we're unhappy about in a peaceful manner. This is the mark of a strong and mature Christian.

Paul says this in his letter to the Romans:

"We who are strong have an obligation to bear with the failings of the weak, and not to please ourselves. Let each of us please his neighbor for his good, to build him up." (Romans 15:1-2)

Paul is describing how Christian relationships are to work. Bear with the failings of your fellow Christians, whom you probably perceive to be weaker in the faith than you are. By doing so, you prove that you're strong. That means doing exactly what Paul has written here in the book of Philippians:

"Do nothing from selfish ambition or conceit, but in humility count others more significant than yourselves. Let each of you look not only to his own interests, but also to the interests of others." (Philippians 2:3-4)

See, these types of things don't come easy or naturally. We don't automatically put others first. Our initial inclination is always to put ourselves first. We are selfish to the core, and Paul makes it clear that it's a weakness of ours—it's something that prevents us from growing in Christ's likeness, if we're not careful, and if we're not intentionally and deliberately denying ourselves and taking up our cross, which are two things we must do in order to follow Jesus (Mark 8:34).

This is how we handle conflict in a way that doesn't lead us into sin: we humble ourselves. And by doing so, we do our part for living at peace with other Christians. And when we're offended by someone, which WILL happen at some point or another, we humble ourselves, and we go to them. And we pray about it. And we talk about it. And we resolve to preserve our unity, because our unity is an answer to Jesus' prayer to the Father than we would be one (John 17:11).

I don't know if you've ever viewed conflict with other Christians in light of that prayer, but when we refuse to work things out with a fellow brother or sister in Christ who has offended us, we are in essence saying "no" to this prayer that Jesus made. We're also saying "no" to His commandment that we love one another (John 15:12).

We must remember that being intentionally humble and thinking of others as more important than ourselves will keep us abiding in Christ, producing the fruit of gentleness and self-control. When we intentionally maintain our humility in the midst of conflict, we keep our flesh on a short leash, so that it doesn't get the best of us.

This is what Paul was talking about when he wrote:

"Have this mind among yourselves, which is yours in Christ Jesus," (Philippians 2:5)

That brings us to our next point, which is that Jesus Himself gave us the biblical blueprint for conflict resolution.

Jesus Gave Us the Biblical Blueprint For Conflict Resolution

This brings us to one of the greatest passages in all of Scripture. The passage we're about to read reveals some of the greatest, richest truths that have ever confronted the human mind. We must see this passage in light of the context of conflict. Of course, the conflict that God had with humanity could not have been resolved by us, because the resolution of humanity's conflict with God required a mediator—but who among us could ever qualify? None of us, on our own, can approach God, and in fact the Scriptures reveal that if it were not for God's saving grace, none of us WOULD approach God. Not because we wouldn't be so brave, but because on our own, we're so radically corrupted. We cannot escape the fact that on our own, apart from God's redeeming grace, we're self-centered and self-focused. That's just how desperately corrupt the unregenerate nature is.

The way that we resolve conflict peacefully is to take on the mindset of Christ, Paul writes. And he continues, writing:

"Who, though He was in the form of God, did not count equality with God a thing to be grasped, but emptied Himself, by taking the form of a servant, being born in the likeness of men." (Philippians 2:6-7)

This is such an incredible thing to ponder. He had stood outside of time for all of eternity, but out of love, He left eternity and stepped into human existence. Even though, as John tells us, in the beginning, Jesus was with God and He was God, and He created everything that has ever come into existence (John 1:1-3), He did not count equality with God as a thing to be grasped. What a stark contrast this is to Adam, who viewed equality with God as a thing to covet, to desire, to pursue, and to bring within his grasp. Jesus didn't stop being God—He didn't lose His divine nature (just like we can't lose our human nature). Instead, He took on a new nature—a human nature—for the sake of being like us so that He could be a mediator before God for us.

When conflict arises and tempers get flared up and people stop thinking reasonably because they're overcome by the emotion of anger, the first thing we must do is follow Christ's example, and relinquish our personal rights. That means stepping down from our proverbial throne and surrendering our individual right to be offended or upset, and you do it for the sake of making peace. Because if Jesus could do it for the sake of making peace with us, how dare we refuse to do the same on a much smaller scale for the sake of making peace with a brother or sister in Christ! This is what true humility looks like.

"And being found in human form, He humbled himself by becoming obedient to the point of death, even death on a cross." (Philippians 2:8)

There is no denying the fact that the world handles conflict by looking for some type of compromise. The Christian handles conflict with self-sacrificial forgiveness, just as it was necessary for Jesus to sacrifice Himself for the sake of forgiving us. Don't miss the fact that He was the One who was offended—the conflict between God and humanity started with us sinning against Him. And yet, He's the One who served as the very sacrifice that His justice required. No matter which side of the conflict you're on, you have a responsibility to own your half of the conflict and to forgive a brother or sister in Christ who has offended you. That means giving up any right you have to be angry for the glory of Christ. The Lord Jesus gladly and willfully surrendered His privileges, becoming a human being in order that He could reconcile the conflict between man and God, which could only be done by dying in our place so that His righteousness could be imputed to us, while our sin was imputed to Him.

You remember how Adam was afraid when He was separated from God for the first time in his short existence? Jesus faced the same thing: the Father had to turn away from Him, leaving Him alone and isolated from the Father for the first and only time.

Have you ever considered the fact that if Jesus had come and lived a full life and died of old age, nothing would have been accomplished, and the conflict between humanity and God would remain unsettled? Jesus was obedient unto death. Our calling is to be obedient to death as well. And so we must take it seriously when the Scriptures encourage us to love and stand united with other Christians. We must first surrender our rights, and secondly, we must be obedient to what God has instructed. Remember these two things when you're tempted to break the bonds of fellowship with a fellow Christian. Because it's impossible to take that step—in which you break off fellowship with another Christian—if you're being humble and obedient; it's as impossible as coming up with 5 by adding 2+2.

And when you take on the mindset of Christ by practicing these two things, God steps in and does His part. If you exalt yourself in the sight of the Lord and refuse to participate in resolving the conflict, you will be humbled—if you're a legitimate child of God. But if, on the other hand, you humble yourself in the sight of the Lord, you will be exalted by Him.

"Therefore God has highly exalted him and bestowed on him the name that is above every name, so that at the name of Jesus every knee should bow, in heaven and on earth and under the earth, and every tongue confess that Jesus Christ is Lord, to the glory of God the Father." (Philippians 2:9-11)

Because of Jesus' humility and obedience to the Father, God has restored and exalted Him highly—so highly that at the Final Judgment, even the most wicked people who ever lived will be forced to stand before Him and acknowledge that He alone is Lord, and that He alone has all authority and the right to rule. Even those who don't belong to Jesus because they have steadfastly rejected Him for all of their earthly lives will be condemned by the very words they will be forced to speak.

Paul tells us that Jesus was given the name that is above every name. What name is that? I think it's pretty easy for us and those in our culture to miss what that means, but the Jews would have known exactly what Paul was referring to, because in the Old Testament, there was one name that was so far above every name, they didn't even dare to speak or pronounce it. It consists of four letters which cannot be pronounced: YHWH. What the Jews would do was take those letters and insert the vowels from the name "Adonai," so that it could be pronounced "Yahweh," which means "Lord." That's why Paul immediately follows that up by telling us that every knee will bow (a sign of submission) and every tongue will confess that Jesus Christ is Lord. He is Yahweh—the name above every name!

Now, of course, God will not exalt you in the same way. But you will be exalted for following Jesus on the path of peaceful conflict resolution. You'll be rewarded with a deeper sense of peace and contentment, and you will see that by resolving the conflict God's way, you've honored Him and brought glory to Him, and you will have grown in Christ's likeness. And for the Christian, there is nothing more exhilarating and rewarding than that!

If you have conflict with a fellow brother or sister in Christ, and you're tempted to sin and break off fellowship with that person, heed the Holy Spirit's advice here, and have this mind—to be humble and obedient before God—which is yours in Christ Jesus.

~~~

Chapter 8: Growing in Obedience

Philippians 2:12-18

I am not the type of person who likes instruction manuals. Early in my marriage, my wife figured out that I am actually probably the least handy person she's ever met. If I buy a product and it comes with an instruction manual, she needs to be the one to figure it out. And if we buy something that requires assembly, she could put the box in the front room, and that thing would just sit there all-year long, if it were up to me. And it's not that I don't want to put it together—I wish I could. The problem is that if the product that comes with the instruction manual says anything beyond, "Flip switch to 'on,'" I just feel like I get bogged down with details. I suppose I just expect everything I buy to be somewhat intuitive, and if it's not . . . well, my wife is really good with instruction manuals.

I think my problem boils down to this: I like to go with my initial instincts when it comes to learning about new things, and when it comes to something that has 15 parts and 50 screws of various sizes, you have to rely on more than instincts.

There is a major misconception about Christianity in our world: many people believe that our faith is old, stale, and based on a 2,000 year old instruction manual, which we call the Bible. As if the Bible is a bunch of do's and don'ts—

and that the Christian life is so filled with rules, it's like walking a tightrope over the Grand Canyon.

The central message of our text today is "work out your salvation with fear and trembling," and what we're going to see is that the Christian faith is not just a bunch of do's and don'ts, but that we were not only saved by grace, but we continue to live by grace, which means learning to be sensitive to the leading of the Holy Spirit. We're about to move very quickly from theological contemplation to real life application. Understanding and reflecting on the great work of Christ on Calvary is important, but its purpose is much more than historical head knowledge. It starts there, but once a person internalizes those truths, it should change absolutely everything; it must have an effect on our lives.

We're coming down from what many might liken to the Mount Everest of Scripture: a pinnacle of sorts, without any doubt. Paul just told us about how Jesus stepped down from His throne in Heaven in order to become one of us, in order that He might resolve the conflict between God and anyone who would trust in Him and the sufficiency of His work on our behalf on the Cross. We saw that this was the blueprint for resolving conflict between Christians, which can be a risky and steep task indeed, because there's no guarantee that if you humble yourself and submit yourself to another person that they will do the same in return. In fact, some people aren't troubled by causing division among Christians at all. What do you do with someone like that? Paul answers that in Romans 16:17, where he writes,

"Watch out for those who cause divisions and create obstacles contrary to the doctrine that you have been taught; avoid them, for such persons do not serve our Lord Christ, but their own appetites." (Romans 16:17b-18a)

If someone will not participate in resolving conflict peacefully and in a Christ-like manner, steer clear of them. That person should consider the possibility that they're not following Jesus. But the fact is that the life that is devoted to Christ will follow in His steps, and will seek to resolve conflict and restore peace. And this involves learning to live in a way that is totally contrary to the flesh.

Do you think that Paul might have something really important to say, right on the heels of this beautiful passage about Jesus? We can be sure that he does.

"Therefore, my beloved, as you have always obeyed, so now, not only as in my presence but much more in my absence, work out your own salvation with fear and trembling, for it is God who works in you, both to will and to work for his good pleasure." (Philippians 2:12-13)

Don't forget that when we begin a passage with the word "therefore," it's a statement that's based on the verses and passages that led up to this point. So when we see the word "therefore," we must reflect on what it's there for. It's there because every knee will bow before Jesus and every tongue will confess that He is Lord (vv. 10-11). It's there because He alone has the name that is above every name (v. 9). It's there because Jesus taught us what it means to humble ourselves by humbling Himself in obedience to the Father (v. 8). It's there because He emptied Himself in order that His Spirit could fill us (v. 7). It's there because if we're in Christ, we should have the mind of Christ (v. 5), being fully capable of humbling ourselves in the same way, doing nothing from selfish ambition or conceit, considering others more important than ourselves, and considering the interests of others in addition to our own interests (vv. 3-4).

110

Paul is saying that when we consider these truths, it should change absolutely everything for us. When we consider these truths, we see both the importance and the beauty of denying ourselves. Because we have the mind of Christ, we must resist the temptation to look to ourselves, and instead, we must look to the Cross. Because God has given us this mind, there is a clear implication that we must adopt this mindset as our own.

The more we adopt this mindset, the more we must learn to obey. That's the first practical application of the truths that have led us to this point. "Obey what," you might ask. That's a good question. What are we supposed to obey? A bunch of rules and regulations? A bunch of do's and don'ts? Paul leaves this question unanswered, but he does give us a hint or two. He reflects back on the obedience he initially saw in them back when he was with them in Philippi, and he tells them that they have continued in their growth in obedience in his absence. Thus, to answer this question, we have to understand what they were obedient to in his presence, and the answer to that is "obedience to the gospel," and living in a manner that is worthy of the gospel. It means knowing that Jesus is Lord of all, and doing something with that knowledge: living it out. It means taking the same attitude that Paul has: to live is Christ!

When Paul commends them for their obedience, he means that they're living a life that reflects the grace that they've been given. It means that they're living in recognition of the fact that they are not their own, but that they've been bought at a high price. See, there's an outworking in our lives of God's in-working, and it starts with obedience. God changes our hearts from a heart of stone to a heart of living flesh. This alone enables us to respond to Him in obedience. And so when a person refuses to be obedient—that is, when their life is lived for the sake of selfish

111

ambition and selfish desires—something is very wrong, because where there is no outward evidence of an internal change, all one can do is wonder if a person has truly been regenerated. That's why Jesus says that you'll know a good tree by its fruit, because bad trees don't produce good fruit, and good trees don't produce bad fruit.

The type of obedience that Paul is talking about entails producing good fruit—the fruit of the Spirit—and no longer producing bad fruit, which is what we see in a person who is still living according to the desires of the flesh. What might that include?

"The works of the flesh are evident: sexual immorality, impurity, sensuality, idolatry, sorcery, enmity, strife, jealousy, fits of anger, rivalries, dissensions, divisions, envy, drunkenness, orgies, and things like these." (Galatians 5:19-21)

That sounds a lot like Las Vegas, doesn't it? They don't call it "Sin City" for nothing! Vegas is famous because you can find those types of things without a whole lot of effort. But quite honestly, you can find these things and indulge yourself in them anywhere you go. Paul isn't saying that we won't be tempted by these things. We will be. He's not even saying we won't occasionally stumble and fall into sin. But don't be content with them! Don't grow comfortable with these things. Repent immediately! If a person continues to exhibit these types of things, and there's no struggle against these things, then of course there is no obedience. And where there is no obedience, it's either because someone is stifling the work that the Holy Spirit is doing in their life, or it's because the Holy Spirit isn't present in their life at all.

You see, when trials come and life gets difficult, it's tempting and it's easy to look for an easier way. We can be sure that we will face the temptation to think, "I'll just take care of this my way, and then I'll come back to doing things the way God wants me to do things." Obedience takes work (especially in the midst of trials), and Paul's instruction to work—to be willfully obedient to the way that the Lord would have you go—isn't going to be extremely popular in a world that values things like independence, autonomy, having fun, and doing things differently. Paul's instruction is to do things the same way—repeatedly, when necessary—that Jesus did things.

So Paul instructs us to work out our salvation with fear and trembling. This is a tricky phrase, because it sounds like Paul's saying that in some sense we must work for our salvation. But we must know that there are different types of salvation. There's salvation which is freedom from the penalty of sin—that's justification. There's salvation which is freedom from the power of sin—that's sanctification. Finally, there is freedom from the presence of sin—that's glorification. The question, then, is which sense Paul is referring to. He's obviously not talking about justification. In Galatians, he emphatically and clearly states that by the works of the law, none will be justified (Galatians 2:16). He's not talking about glorification, either; that will happen one day when we stand before Jesus and see Him as He really is (1st John 3:2).

Sanctification, however, is different. Sanctification is the aspect of salvation that we're working out in the present moment for the Christian. The leading of the Holy Spirit is the means by which we are separated from the power of sin. We participate in this aspect of salvation, how? By being—you guessed it—obedient to His leading in our lives.

So what does it mean to "work out" our salvation? It means let your light shine! Don't keep it hidden. Your life is meant to be an outward reflection of the inward reality of the presence and the work of the Holy Spirit. Why must we do it with fear and trembling? I think the answer is found in one of my favorite proverbs:

"The fear of the LORD is the beginning of wisdom." (Proverbs 9:10)

Without a healthy dose of the fear of the Lord, we will not be sensitive to the leading of the Holy Spirit. Without a healthy dose of the fear of the Lord, we will not be obedient to what He leads us to do. Without a healthy dose of the fear of the Lord, we will be led by our flesh, and not by the Holy Spirit. This is not a fear that leads us to despair, however; rather, this is a fear that leads us to a greater sense of personal holiness. This is a fear that teaches us not to become arrogant, overly confident, or overly self-reliant, but to be humble and gentle in spirit. This is a fear that leads us to become more and more like Christ. This is a fear that gives us a reason to hope, because it gives evidence of our sanctification, which is the only proof anyone can have of their justification.

The reason that our salvation—our sanctification—must be worked out with fear and trembling is because if you are in Christ, God is ever present within you, and that means that He's there with you when the trials and difficulties of life come your way. In fact—and you may not like this fact—the truth is that He may have led you right into those trials and difficulties, just so He could teach you how to handle it in a way that honors Him. Part of our sanctification is learning how to resolve conflict with a fellow brother or sister in Christ, because when we resolve conflict in a way that honors God (which means handling it His way instead of our way), it illustrates the message and the power of the Gospel.

The difficulty, when we face trials in life, is that we're not all just a bunch of robots without a free will of our own. It's not like God programmed a code into us that will work perfectly every time, because we have no way of overriding it. How do we handle the various trials and tribulations that we face, knowing that the Bible doesn't speak explicitly on a lot of the issues we face in life? There's a school of thought that says "Speak where the Bible speaks, and be silent where the Bible is silent," but did you know that the Bible has nothing explicit to say about handling a loved one who has a drug addiction? Did you know that the Bible has nothing to say about using your telephone to call someone who is sick? Notice that Paul doesn't specifically tell them, step by step, what these people who are facing strife and division are supposed to do.

This brings us back to the misconception that the Bible is a book that's full of do's and don'ts. The Bible does not serve that purpose in the life of the Christian. The Bible tells us to follow the leading of the Holy Spirit, who will lead us and direct us. See, God has saved us by His grace through faith, and He dwells within us—the Bible tells us that much—but we still have to live and we still have to make difficult choices. But we have a secret source of life and direction and wisdom in the fact that the Holy Spirit is living in us and helping us when we're confronted with difficult choices.

So often, we're tempted to live as if we've been left on our own to make the tough choices and to deal with the difficult circumstances, but Paul is reminding us that that's not true—the God who sent His Son to die for us has sent

His Holy Spirit to dwell within us, to lead us, to guide us, to teach us, to shape and mold us. The question is: are you sensitive to His leading?

See, here's where we see the difference between the legalist and the person who is living by grace. The legalist believes that everything is wrong unless the Bible specifically and explicitly says it's permissible. The person who walks by grace, on the other hand, has a much different view. They believe that everything is permissible unless the Holy Spirit leads them otherwise. As a side note, the Holy Spirit will always lead us in accordance with the Scriptures; never against them. That means you're free to live and choose in accordance with the way that the Holy Spirit is directing your conscience, understanding what Paul said to the Corinthians:

"All things are lawful, but not all things are helpful. All things are lawful, but not all things build up." (1st Corinthians 10:23)

Elsewhere, in Romans 14, Paul emphasizes the importance of acting in accordance with the leading of the Holy Spirit, and this is what he comes to in verse 23: "For whatever does not proceed from faith is sin."

Our confidence for dealing with the difficult seasons and trials of life must be based firmly in the presence of Jesus through the Holy Spirit in our lives. We are in Him, and He is in us, and we are never left on our own to figure things out. He's living through us, and we're living in Him, and all we can fully rely on is His love for us and the work that He has done and is doing in our lives. When we can learn to be obedient to that much, we're ready to experience a fuller expression of obedience, which looks like this:

"Do all things without grumbling or disputing, that you may be blameless and innocent, children of God without blemish in the midst of a crooked and twisted generation, among whom you shine as lights in the world."
(Philippians 2:14-15)

Here, Paul is basically returning to the root of the issues that the Philippians were facing. They were grumbling. They were having disputes with one another. And Paul puts the solution in crystal clear language for us: do everything without grumbling or disputing. Don't argue! Quit your bickering! He sounds like a parent, doesn't he? The Israelites grumbled as they were being led to the Promised Land—and God rightfully judged them for it. In Exodus 16:2, we read, "And the whole congregation of the people of Israel grumbled against Moses and Aaron in the wilderness." That's almost comical. Can you imagine about a million people openly grumbling about you as a leader? We think it's bad when two or three people grumble against us—at least I do. But with one sentence, Moses turns the whole thing around and gives the people what might be likened to a verbal pile-driver. In verse 8, Moses says, "Your grumbling is not against us but against the LORD."

You see, what grumbling really reveals is a dissatisfaction and a distrust in the Lord Himself. It demonstrates that a person doesn't really believe that the Holy Spirit is working in them to strengthen and guide them through trials. It demonstrates a disbelief in the promise that God is working all things to the good of those who are called according to His purposes. It shows that a person doesn't believe that the grace of God is sufficient to get them through any trial or tribulation.

117

And all of this is very significant, because, as Paul points out here, when we grumble and complain and argue with and about one another, the world cannot see the light and the life of Christ within us. Now we see what the real cost of selfish ambition is. Here we see that self-exaltation is not without consequence. The truth is that selfishness, as demonstrated through grumbling and disputing, leaves those who are lost in the darkness just as they are. And so when we're tempted to bicker with and complain about other Christians, this is the reality check we need. See, if you respond to an offense by a fellow Christian with grumbling and complaining, what kind of a witness will that be to the world, who, by the way, does the exact same thing when they're upset? What's the difference between the way you handle conflict and the way that they do? Unless there is something supernatural about the way you handle conflict and the way love and forgive other Christians when they offend you, Paul is saying that there is nothing you have to offer to the world in terms of your witness. There should be something about each one of us that this crooked and twisted generation has no explanation for other than to say, "God is the only explanation."

A life that is constantly led and being transformed by the power and workings of the Holy Spirit can be a powerful witness of the Gospel to the world, but complaining and arguing about other Christians will dim and greatly diminish the light that has been given to us.

The third expression of obedience is found in verses 16-18, and is seen as a by-product of our refusal to grumble or complain, and therefore the witness of our light is shining brightly for the world to see.

"Holding fast to the word of life, so that in the Day of Christ I may be proud that I did not run in vain or labor in

118

vain. Even if I am to be poured out as a drink offering upon the sacrificial offering of your faith, I am glad and rejoice with you all. Likewise you also should be glad and rejoice with me." (Philippians 2:16-18)

There is a life that is lived for absolutely nothing, and there is a life that is radically different which is not lived for nothing. The things that we do out of vanity and selfish ambition ultimately are all done in vain. The only things that have eternal significance are the things that are done out of a loving obedience to God and a love for our neighbors—especially for those who are our fellow brothers and sisters in Christ.

Like Paul, we should be living every day of our lives in anticipation of the day when we stand before the Lord, and our every deed is laid out for inspection, and the things which are done for the glory of Christ out of a willful and devoted obedience to Him will be like the finest jewels, which will be displayed for all to see.

Paul writes this to the Corinthians: "Now if anyone builds on the foundation (which is the Lord Jesus Christ) with gold, silver, precious stones, wood, hay, straw— each one's work will become manifest, for the Day will disclose it, because it will be revealed by fire, and the fire will test what sort of work each one has done. If the work that anyone has built on the foundation survives, he will receive a reward. If anyone's work is burned up, he will suffer loss, though he himself will be saved, but only as through fire."

Some will come enter into heaven smelling like they just came from a bonfire, because while they belonged to Jesus, their works were not done for the glory of God, and they'll all be burned up. Some will come into heaven, and their works will withstand the fire, because they were done purely out of selfless submission and obedience to the Holy Spirit for the glory of Christ. What's the difference between the two? Paul tells us that the difference is "holding fast to the word of life." What does that mean? It must be seen as a contrast to grumbling and disputing. Grumbling and disputing cause our witness to vanish. Thus, instead of being preoccupied with grumbling and disputing with one another, we must remain focused on proclaiming the word of life, which is the Gospel message. Holding fast to the word of life means remaining humbly obedient to the life of Christ in us, faithfully proclaiming the good news, and thus shining the light of Christ into this dark, dark world.

This is simply another way of exhorting the Philippians (and us) to live in a manner that is worthy of the Gospel of Jesus Christ, and reminding us that living in any other manner is all done in vain.

Paul says that even if he's going to be poured out like a sacrificial drink offering, he will rejoice just in knowing that the Philippians are holding fast to the word of life, and they can rejoice with him. Paul knows that there is a good chance that he'll be put to death. But it's not in vain—it's not all for nothing—if it's what happens because he has held fast to the word of life, being faithfully obedient to the leading of the Holy Spirit. The point here is that if Paul can rejoice over his self-sacrificial obedience to Christ, then the Philippians can rejoice for the same reason, knowing that whether they live or die, Christ will be exalted and glorified in their lives. There is a joy that this brings, knowing that God is glorified through our obedience, which overrides anything and everything which would otherwise cause us to feel afraid or intimidated.

We read in the book of Hebrews about the joy that Jesus felt as He was about to be nailed to the Cross. We read that Jesus, "for the joy that was set before him, endured the cross, despising the shame, and is seated at the right hand of the throne of God." We might be tempted to think, "Why did He feel joy as He looked to the cross that He was about to die on?" It was the same reason that Paul rejoiced: He anticipated with joy the fact that people whose lives would otherwise have been destroyed by the effects of sin will experience forgiveness and newness of life in Christ. Paul could rejoice—and the Philippians could rejoice with him—because His life was humbly given for the sake of serving others and doing the will of God.

Joining with one another and loving one another well by the power of the Holy Spirit out of a desire to be obedient to Christ gives us every reason we need to rejoice. We are His people, and even in the trials and difficulties of life, we can rejoice because Jesus is enough to see us through, and He will never leave or give up on His people.

~~~

Chapter 9: A Legacy of Selflessness

Philippians 2:19-30

It's always interesting to learn about new Biblical characters. The fact that there are so many people mentioned throughout epistles of the New Testament of whom we know so little is a reminder that letters like this letter to the church in Philippi was a real letter written to real people who were dealing with real issues. In our passage today, we're going to learn about two men—one of whom we know quite a bit, and one of whom we know almost nothing.

In the verses that have led us to our passage at hand, Paul talked about how, even though he was facing the real possibility of martyrdom, he was rejoicing because he had poured his life out for the sake of serving others. He hadn't lived for nothing; his life had not been lived in vain—in fact, he had lived for the only thing that truly matters, which is the glory of God by the spreading of the Gospel.

I would argue that it would be impossible to look at Paul's life and come to the honest conclusion that Paul was never a risk-taker. Paul was a major risk-taker. I don't know if anyone in the Bible had a more adventurous life than he did. He strikes me as the kind of guy who was always on the go, and I believe that that's because he realized that this world is not his home. By the time his life was almost over, he had learned a very important lesson: to cling to nothing but Jesus. He wrote to Timothy, "we brought nothing into the world, and we cannot take anything out of the world" (1st Timothy 6:7). Knowing that nothing in this world is worth pursuing more than Jesus, Paul lived for the things that matter in eternity—the things that matter to God—and was going to make the most of his earthly life, and that involved taking risks.

One of the hardest risks to make is investing in people. When we invest in people, there's always the chance that we'll feel burned or cheated in some way. Paul knew what that was all about. Some of the final words we have from his pen record the fact that several people he had invested in had abandoned him in his final hour. He tells Timothy, "Do your best to come to me soon, for Demas, in love with this present world, has deserted me and gone to Thessalonica. Crescens has gone to Galatia, Titus to Dalmatia" (2nd Timothy 4:9-10). We can assume that Crescens and Titus went to their respective destinations in order to minister, but Demas . . . apparently he abandoned Paul and went to Thessalonica to pursue worldly treasure. You get the sense that Paul is somewhat heartbroken about that. He went on to write, "Alexander the coppersmith did me great harm; the Lord will repay him according to his deeds" (v. 14), and then, "At my first defense no one came to stand by me, but all deserted me" (v. 16). Again, we get the sense that Paul felt hurt and abandoned by a lot of the people he had invested his life in.

Relationships are risky, but Paul never hesitated to pour out his life for the sake of serving and discipling others, and because of that, he was able to find plenty of reasons to rejoice even when the going got tough.

The fact that relationships are risky, however, is not an excuse to not invest in people, because the fact of the matter is that obedience to God is risky business. The person who plays it safe and refuses to leave their comfort zone clings to an illusion of safety. Comfort isn't a bad thing, necessarily. Sometimes the Good Shepherd will lead us beside still waters. But don't cling to comfort, because it so easily becomes an idol. The reality is that such an attitude will often lead us into disobedience, because comfort can so easily become a desire of the flesh. Taking risks for Jesus can be dangerous—it can cost us dearly sometimes—but not taking risks for Jesus is even more dangerous.

As we come to the closing passage of chapter two, we're introduced once again to Timothy. Remember that Timothy was mentioned as being present with Paul in the opening sentence of this letter.

"I hope in the Lord Jesus to send Timothy to you soon, so that I too may be cheered by news of you. For I have no one like him, who will be genuinely concerned for your welfare." (Philippians 2:19-20)

The relationship between Paul and Timothy was special. Timothy was like a son to Paul, and Paul had invested years of his life in discipling Timothy. Remember that Paul is in chains in Rome as he writes this letter. He desires to go and see the Philippians himself, but if he can't, he indicates here that he hoped to send Timothy—although he wasn't ready to send Timothy just yet. He was confident that when the time came to send Timothy, Timothy would experience great joy to see that the Philippians had resolved the conflict that they had been facing, and he anticipated the day that Timothy would come back with a positive report.

And I love the reason that Paul gives us for Timothy being the one he would chose to go and visit the Philippians:

because he was the only person who was willing to go who would be as concerned about the spiritual health of the Christians in Philippi as he (Paul) himself was. If we were to translate verse 20 literally, it would say, "For I have no one else equally-minded." What Paul means is that there is nobody but Timothy who resembles Paul in his concern for the welfare of others.

Keep in mind how much Paul loved Timothy. After all, nearly the entire church in Rome had abandoned Paul, but Timothy stood by him. And here's Paul, who knows that he could be dying soon, ready to send his most beloved co-worker to these people. Does Paul need Timothy? I think it's safe to say that, in a sense, he does. He needs Timothy there to deliver messages. He needs Timothy there for companionship. He needs Timothy for encouragement. But he's willing to neglect his own needs for the needs of others. What we see here, in light of all of this, is that Paul is willing to practice what he's been preaching. "Do nothing from selfish ambition or conceit, but in humility count others more significant than yourselves. Let each of you look not only to his own interests, but also to the interests of others" (Philippians 2:3-4).

Of course, right after that, Paul discussed how Jesus was the perfect model of those principles, but now Paul is saying that this is how the Christian life is supposed to work, so he's willing to put his money where his mouth is. He's not just considering his own interests and needs; he's considering the interests and the needs of the Philippians, too.

We need to understand that Timothy's concern for the spiritual health of these Christian Philippians is a concern that mirrors the concern of Christ for his people.

"For they all seek their own interests, not those of Jesus Christ." (Philippians 2:21)

It is so easy for us to chase after our own interests. That's what comes naturally to us. That's where the flesh leads us. But that kind of attitude leads to a legacy of selfishness. Think about this guy, Demas, who was mentioned in the closing of Paul's second letter to Timothy. We know nothing about the guy, other than that he abandoned the faith for the sake of his love of the world.

In the parable of the seed sower, Jesus tells us that some seed will fall among the thorns. Jesus tells us that these seeds represent those who "hear the word, but the cares of the world and the deceitfulness of riches and the desires for other things enter in and choke the word, and it proves unfruitful" (Mark 4:18-19). These are people who received the Gospel with joy, but refused to make it the number one priority in their lives. As a result, they remain unregenerate—these are false conversions. Paul apparently saw quite a few of those in his time, but he knew that such was not the case with Timothy. Like Paul, Timothy was concerned not with his own interests, but with the things which were of interest to Jesus.

There are plenty of things we could list off which are of interest to Jesus, but in this context, the thing that Paul knows that Timothy, like Jesus, would feel concern for is the spiritual health of the Christian community.

I had a discussion this past week with a fellow pastor who didn't feel that it's anyone's business how anyone else is running their church or what they're teaching their congregation. And so, he argued, if one church is teaching or leading falsely, everyone else on the outside should just keep their nose out of it. However, as John MacArthur so eloquently puts it, "Pacifism has never been a pastoral option in the war for people's souls" (http://www.gty.org/Blog/B140227). It is impossible to love Christ's people without feeling a sense of concern for their spiritual health. That's why Paul said to the Corinthians, "there is the daily pressure on me *of* concern for all the churches" (2nd Corinthians 11:28).

Paul and Timothy were concerned for the spiritual welfare of churches like the church in Philippi because Jesus is concerned for the spiritual welfare of His people, as we would expect anyone who claims to be a good shepherd to be concerned for each of his sheep.

"But you know Timothy's proven worth, how as a son with a father he has served with me in the gospel. I hope therefore to send him just as soon as I see how it will go with me, and I trust in the Lord that shortly I myself will come also." (Philippians 2:22-24)

Timothy was like Christ-like in his selflessness. Think about this with me. He was willing to be sent by his father (in this case, his spiritual father, Paul) to do work on Paul's behalf. He was willing to abandon any and all selfish pursuit or ambition for the sake of others. And so we see that Timothy is a model of selflessness, and in that regard, he is an excellent model of Christlikeness. If the Philippians could become a little more like Timothy in this regard, they would also be growing in Christ's likeness.

But here's what we need to understand: Timothy wasn't willing to make all of these selfless sacrifices in order that the Philippians would understand how great he (Timothy) was—that would be acting out of selfish ambition. Instead, he's willing to make these selfless sacrifices because 1) he understands how great Jesus is; and 2) he wants everyone else to see and understand how great Jesus is.

Paul tells us that Timothy had proven himself. We know that Paul had high standards when it came to people in ministry—his standards were so high that he broke off his relationship with Barnabas for a season over John-Mark's participation in their ministry together. His standards were so high that he even got in Peter's face and rebuked him at one point. Paul had high standards—which is a good thing—and Timothy had surpassed those standards. Timothy was faithful and trustworthy.

After ten years of mentoring Timothy, Paul knew that Timothy was up for the task at hand. He had adopted Paul's spiritual DNA. He was as committed to loving and serving Jesus as Paul was, and he was as committed to loving and serving the church as Paul was.

I suppose this is as good a time as any to ask if you've thought about how you're influencing others for Christ. We're all called to make disciples. The question is: how do we best do that? There's really no answer that is universally right for everyone—it depends on a lot of things (your gifting, in particular, but also your living situation, your job, etc.), but it's nevertheless something that we're all called to do. But I will say this much: it will almost always involve something as simple as living out your Christian faith so that those who are closest to you can see what it's all about. You know what that means? It means you can't really make disciples over the internet. Just so we're clear. My friend Jamie and I were recently talking about the pros and cons of streaming church services online, and we both reached the same conclusion: it would be too tempting for many people to substitute an online experience for in-person fellowship, which really is no substitute.

Now, I understand that a lot of people get a little nervous and uncomfortable when we start talking about the importance of discipleship, because so many people hold this notion that we have to be perfected as a disciple ourselves before we disciple others. There would be no disciples, if that were the case. Part of how I disciple my own kids is to own up to my failures as soon as I see them. Those of us who are parents need to understand that we are constantly leaving an impression on our kids, especially while they're still living at home. If our walk with the Lord is a secondary issue for us (or worse), they will not grow up with an understanding of how important it is to make our walk with the Lord our top priority. Our kids (like anyone who is close to us) have a pretty good idea of what's really going on behind the curtain in Oz, if you know what I mean. And so we've got to demonstrate an authentic love and obedience to the Lord, and the only way we will truly demonstrate that is to actually cultivate it in our own lives.

And even if you're not a biological parent, you can always be a parent in the faith to someone. That's how Paul describes his relationship with Timothy. They had spent a vast amount of time together, and Paul had invested in Timothy. He had allowed Timothy to get close enough to see that Paul's faith was an authentic faith. And because of all of these things, Paul was able to build Timothy up in his faith. That's what discipleship is all about, ultimately. So before we move on, let me simply challenge each of you to consider what kind of a spiritual imprint you're leaving on those who are consistently closest to you as you go about your daily routine. Where did Timothy learn to be like Jesus in his selflessness? He learned it from Paul, through the power of the Holy Spirit working in Him.

Paul wasn't able to send Timothy just yet, however. Paul tells us that he wanted to keep Timothy by his side until he saw how it went with him. In other words, he wanted to wait until his case was decided. For that reason, the time was not quite right for Timothy to go and visit the Philippians (although we can be certain that Paul would have sent him if the circumstances had been less pressing).

There was, however, someone else Paul had in mind; someone who knew the Philippians and could do what Paul was incapable of doing, being that he was imprisoned.

"I have thought it necessary to send to you Epaphroditus, my brother and fellow worker and fellow soldier, and your messenger and minister to my need." (Philippians 2:25)

Epaphroditus is one of those characters that we know very, very little about. In fact, he's never mentioned anywhere outside of Paul's letter to the Philippians. In 4:18, we'll see that Epaphroditus is actually the man who had been sent by the Philippians to deliver a gift to Paul on their behalf. So it's possible, if not likely, that he was an elder with the church in Philippi. Whatever the case, the Philippians knew and trusted Epaphroditus, as evidenced by the fact that they trusted him to safely deliver their financial gift to Paul. But Paul is not simply sending Epaphroditus back home. Rather, when we consider the four words that Paul uses to describe Epaphroditus, we'll catch a glimpse of the type of man he was.

First, Paul refers to him as his "brother." Paul had probably never met Epaphroditus before he had come to deliver this gift to Paul; he had probably become a Christian under the leadership of the Philippian church. And yet, Paul refers to him as a "brother," referring to the fact that they share the source of life that they had in common in Christ Jesus. Having ministered to Paul, Paul had had a chance to see the heart, the faith, and the fruit that was being produced in life

130

of Epaphroditus. If Paul had had any doubts regarding the legitimacy of Epaphroditus' faith, we can be sure that he would not refer to him as a "brother," and that he wouldn't have sent him to the Philippian church on his (Paul's) behalf.

Secondly, Paul refers to him as a "fellow worker." The Greek word that Paul uses is *synergos*, the word from which we get the English word "synergy," which is defined by the Merriam-Webster Dictionary as "the increased effectiveness that results when two or more people or businesses work together." They shared common goals and interests, and they made each other better at what they did.

Thirdly, Paul refers to Epaphroditus as a "fellow soldier." We often forget that we're constantly engaged in a spiritual battle, and there is no place like being in the trenches in ministry. When you are engaged in physical warfare, your best friend is the soldier who stands next to you. You encourage one another. You challenge and motivate one another. You lift one another's spirits when the other is feeling low. It is no different in the trenches of ministry. It can be a lonely place to be. Feelings of insecurity, vulnerability, and inadequacy run rampant. It is wonderful to know that there are "fellow soldiers" in the trenches with us to encourage, challenge, and motivate us. Paul had someone who could be that type of person for him in Epaphroditus.

Fourth and finally, Paul refers to him as "your messenger." The Greek word means "ambassador," and implies that he represents someone else. In this case, he represented the Philippians, but he also, in a sense, represented Jesus. Jesus uses His people to serve His people on His behalf. That requires a steadfast commitment to—here's that word again—selflessness. That's the type of man Epaphroditus

131

was. That's why Paul was desiring to send him to the Philippians.

What's amazing to me is that we can know this much about someone who is mentioned only in passing in God's word. We see that he, like Timothy, was a selfless servant of others. And that got me thinking—how would Paul describe me? Or better yet, how would God describe me? See, we tend to focus on the negative. I might be tempted to think that God would look at me as a complete sinner or as someone who is double-minded and duplicitous. But when He looks at us through the blood of Christ, I don't think He gets as hung up on our weaknesses as we do. He sees us as His beloved people, whom He sent His only Son Jesus to redeem. He sees us and loves us as His children. Most Christians know that God loves them the way that someone who has read all of the books in the world on swimming, and yet has never tried actually swimming, knows about swimming. Do we deserve God's love? No, we are brought into His Kingdom by His grace, through faith in the Son He sent for the sake of bearing His wrath against sin on our behalf. And yet we still struggle to believe that we're that precious and that valuable to Him. It's okay to struggle with that. I don't know if we can fully comprehend it in this life. But the more we do, the more amazing we see His grace to be, and the more we grow in our love and obedience to Him.

So the reason that Paul would send Epaphroditus to the Philippians on his behalf is because he's a brother, he's a fellow worker, a fellow soldier, and an ambassador (or messenger). But there's an additional reason.

"For he has been longing for you all and has been distressed because you heard that he was ill. Indeed he was ill, near to death. But God had mercy on him, and not only

on him but on me also, lest I should have sorrow upon sorrow. I am the more eager to send him, therefore, that you may rejoice at seeing him again, and that I may be less anxious." (Philippians 2:26-28)

Apparently word had somehow gotten back to the Philippians that Epaphroditus was extremely sick—nearly to the point of death. And then, somehow he got word that they had gotten word, and he was beside himself with anxiety that they would be worried about him. Paul tells us that he "has been distressed" upon learning of what the Philippians had heard of his illness. Some would think that it's great to know that people are concerned with their well-being, but apparently Epaphroditus had recognized the vanity and worthlessness of any type of self-interest. Surely he appreciated their prayers and their concern while he was ill, but now that he was recovered, the last thing he wanted was to be a distraction to the Philippians. The desire to not draw attention to one's self is another great mark of selflessness. Once again, his concern is not primarily for himself—it's for others. With Epaphroditus, it's to the point where he's distraught over the fact that people are focusing their concern and their attention on him.

For all of these reasons, Paul sends Epaphroditus to them. He would be the one to a) minister to them in Paul's (and Timothy's) absence for the time being; and b) deliver this letter to the Philippians.

"So receive him in the Lord with all joy, and honor such men, for he nearly died for the work of Christ, risking his life to complete what was lacking in your service to me." (Philippians 2:29-30)

What we find here is the ultimate picture of selflessness, as Paul tells us that Epaphroditus was willing to risk his life for the sake of doing the work of Christ. The Greek word for "risking" literally means "to not regard" or "to not take into account." That's how he felt regarding his own life in comparison to others. And that's how Jesus felt about His rightful position in Heaven when it came to us (v. 6). In other words, Paul is saying that Epaphroditus was willing to expose himself to the very real possibility of danger for the sake of Christ.

Friends, the Christian life involves taking risks; it is not about playing it safe and staying comfortable. John Piper wrote a book titled, "Risk is Right," and writes, "The Christian life is a call to risk. You either live with risk or waste your life." You see, the Christian life is not about playing things safe and staying tucked away in our comfort zone. Rather, it's about selflessly serving and investing in others, giving ourselves away, and that can't be done properly from the confines of our comfort zones.

If I were to give a sermon titled "How to Waste Your Life," I'd start with this: don't take any risks! Whatever you do, play it safe at all costs! Stay tucked away in your comfort zone, where you'll be comfy and cozy and won't disrupt or disturb anyone else.

When Jesus told the parable of the talents, He told of how two servants took great risks in order to be good stewards of what the Master had given them, while a third servant refuses to risk, and was consequently condemned as being wicked. Why did the two servants take risks, while the third one didn't? It's because the faithful servants had two - attitudes that the wicked servant did not.

First, the faithful stewards trusted in the goodness of the Master. Do you trust in the Master's goodness? Then don't be afraid to be ambitious. Jesus did not hang on a cross so that we could be comfortable and ignore the community around us. As D.L. Moody once said, "If God be your partner, make large plans!"

Secondly, the faithful stewards desired to please the Master. You get the sense that the faithful servants couldn't wait to show the Master what they had done with the talents that had been entrusted with them. Do you desire to please God above anything else?

So here's the challenge: where are you taking risks for Jesus? Where is God calling you to obey and follow Him? Or how about this: what would you not risk for the sake of Jesus? Your house? Your money? Your popularity or your standing before others? What if the Holy Spirit is leading you to share the Gospel with a co-worker? Would you obey? What if He was leading you to go on your first mission trip, or to adopt a child, or simply getting more involved in church? Would you risk your time, energy, and resources? Are you holding what you have with a clenched fist in hopes that God never takes it away from you? Or are you holding what you have with an open hand? Would you be willing to take the attitude that you hold nothing more precious and dear than the work of Christ, both in and through you? The opportunities will vary from one person to another, but the principle is this: we live with risk for the sake of what is eternal or we waste our lives on what is temporary.

Jim Elliot is one of the most famous missionaries of all time. He was also a risk-taker. He abandoned all selfish pursuit and instead teamed up with four other missionaries to bring the Gospel message to a tribe of Ecuadorians known as the Huaoranis. The Huaoranis were a savage group of people who avoided any and all contact with modern society, and so when these missionaries approached them to share the Gospel with them, Jim Elliot and the other missionaries were all speared to death. They took a risk for Christ. Did they win or did they lose that risk? The world would say that they failed, but the Bible tells us that to live is Christ, and to die is gain. So they gained in that sense. But their deaths were also widely publicized, which led to a world-wide effort to bring the Gospel to the Huaoranis, which ultimately resulted in many of them coming to Christ.

Years earlier while Jim was a student in Bible college, he wrote these famous words: "He is no fool who gives what he cannot keep, to save what he cannot lose." Living in obedience means taking risks for the glory of Christ, and it's the only thing worth living for. Everything else slips through our fingers when this life ends.

When Jesus claims a person as His own, that person receives the Holy Spirit. Your nature is replaced, but your personality and your individual will are not. Gradually, over time, He shows us how worthless our ego is—usually by crushing it—and He wages war against that part of us that desires to be the center of attention, and He replaces it with a desire to glorify Christ by selflessly serving others. What a wonderful illustration the lives of Paul, Timothy, and Epaphroditus are of this principle. The Christian life is ultimately about selflessly loving Jesus and glorifying Him by selflessly serving His people, regardless of the risks that may be involved. Jesus is the only thing and the only Person worth risking anything and everything for.

~~~

Chapter 10: The Futility of the Flesh

Philippians 3:1-7

There was a very disturbing study that was released last year, which revealed that about 70 percent of the American population is on at least one prescription drug. That number is somewhat staggering, especially when one realizes what the majority of those prescriptions are supposed to be treating. Prescriptions aren't necessarily a bad thing. If you have allergies which prevent you from breathing, you may need prescription allergy medicine. So before I say anything else, let me be clear that I'm not necessarily opposed to prescriptions. But what disturbs me about the 70 percent is that the second most common prescription is for anti-depressants. Now, don't get me wrong: some people need to be on antidepressant medications because they have an underlying physiological issue. But in a report released in 2011 by the National Center for Health Statistics, it was revealed that the rate of antidepressant use in this country among teens and adults had increased by almost 400% between 1988–1994 and 2005–2008.

Few would doubt that the number of people on antidepressants shot up dramatically in the years since

2008, as our country has been buried deep in a recession. According to Dr. Mark van Ommeren, of the World Health Organisation's department of mental health and substance abuse, "A lot of people are getting antidepressants who shouldn't be getting them." So why are so many people being given prescriptions for antidepressants when they don't have a physiological need for them? Well, part of it could probably be attributed to the fact that there's a mentality that we should be able to take a pill for just about anything. Part of it might have to do with the incentives and kickbacks that doctors get for writing prescriptions. But I would be willing to bet that part of it has to do with consumer demands—if one doctor doesn't give them something that solves their problem, they'll take their business elsewhere.

There's a part of us that desires to experience joyfulness, which is something that we far too often confuse with happiness. But as we've already established earlier in our study of the book of Philippians, happiness is an emotion which is based on our circumstances. Happiness is an emotion, but we must make the choice to rejoice. We would be wise to note that the Bible never tells us to "be happy" in the imperative tense, but that it certainly does tell us to rejoice—yes, in the imperative tense. That's because you can't command someone to feel a certain way. As Christians, joy is a decision that we make which stems from knowing and being known by Jesus, and having a deep trust in Him. That means that it cannot be based on our circumstances . . . or anything else that this world has to offer, for that matter—that's the only explanation for why Paul would develop the theme of rejoicing throughout a letter that was written when he was facing the real possibility of death.

Having just become familiar with two of Paul's friends—Timothy and Epaphroditus—in the text that has led us to this point, Paul will now turn his attention to warning the Ephesians to avoid the tendency to look for joy in the desires of the flesh. After all, it wasn't too far back that he told his readers to rejoice with him (Philippians 2:18). The question is: what should be the basis of their rejoicing? Much of the third chapter is going to be spent answering that question. And so Paul continues, writing,

"Finally, my brethren, rejoice in the Lord." (Philippians 3:1a)

It's a little confusing that this chapter begins with the word "finally," being that this is only the beginning of the third chapter—Paul has almost two whole chapters to go! But the Greek word doesn't express the sense that Paul is nearing his conclusion. Rather, what it means is, "regarding the rest." We might ask, "The rest of what?" The answer is: anything. In other words, Paul is saying, "Whatever issues or problems you have, and regardless of whether you're in the midst of good or bad circumstances, rejoice in the Lord." As John MacArthur notes, "It is a word of transition, not conclusion, since half of Philippians follows it."

Rejoice in the Lord. You know, that's such a short sentence, it's almost automatic for it to slip right by us without receiving a whole lot of our attention. But what exactly does it mean? What does it mean to rejoice? Does it mean that I feel so happy that I can't help but smile? Does it mean that we should never feel grief, sadness, or despair? Just reading this verse might give some a sense of despair, because they're not sure what it even means to rejoice in the Lord!

As we look at this text, we'll find some very helpful clues, which should help us to gain a deeper understanding of what this means.

The first clue is that this is written in the imperative tense. That implies a few very important things. First of all, it implies that it's something we must willfully choose; it's not something that's automatic. It also implies that this isn't just a suggestion. Paul isn't giving a first-century rendition of "If You're Happy and You Know It." He's saying that this is something that we must make the deliberate decision to do, which means that it can't be based on our circumstances.

The fact that this is not something that's just optional for us means that it's really a matter of trusting and obeying the Lord. God's word instructs us to do it. And sometimes, it's really easy to obey this instruction—especially when life is going well. When things are going our way, it's natural for us to feel a victorious sense of joy. But what about the rest of the time? What about when things aren't going well for us.

Let's remember that Paul wrote in the previous chapter that we should do all things without grumbling or complaining. The antithesis of these things is rejoicing. Remember that grumbling and complaining really reveals a distrust in God's sovereign power and purposes, as the Israelites so clearly illustrated as they were being led through the wilderness. Thus, we must understand that to rejoice, in a Biblical sense, means to find contentment and trust in God. It means remembering that He's got the situation under control, and that nothing in our lives is accidental—God is causing (note the active tense of that word) ALL things to work together for the good of those who love Him, and who are therefore called according to His purposes.

Paul had learned to rejoice even in the midst of hardships and trials. In the opening verses of his second letter to the Corinthians, he wrote that, "We do not want you to be unaware, brothers, of the affliction we experienced in Asia. For we were so utterly burdened beyond our strength that we despaired of life itself. Indeed, we felt that we had received the sentence of death. But that was to make us rely not on ourselves but on God who raises the dead" (2nd Corinthians 1:8-9).

Trials very well may cause us to despair or to feel grief or sorrow. But beneath the surface, we must learn to trust and abide in the steadfast faithfulness of the Lord. Think of it like a submarine in the midst of a storm. There can be a hurricane going by on the surface of the sea, but those in the submarine that's submerged a few hundred feet down wouldn't notice a thing.

Rejoicing in the Lord does not mean experiencing a superficial happiness or exuberance on the surface which is based on good circumstances. Rather, it means trusting that God is sovereign, and because He's sovereign and all-powerful, He either causes or allows everything that comes to pass, and He's using every circumstance we find ourselves in to teach us to grow in our walk with Him.

It's also worth noting that Paul tells us to rejoice *in the Lord*. To rejoice as the Holy Spirit is instructing us through Paul's pen requires that we first be in the Lord. What does it mean to be "in the Lord"? It means that He's the source of our life. It means that He's the foundation we stand on. It means that He's living in us and through us. It means our lives are so intertwined with the life of Jesus that we cannot bear the thought of living without Him.

We need to understand an important distinction between what Paul is telling us and what the world offers us through the fields of pop psychology and positive thinking. This is not about positive thinking as much as it's about right thinking. It's about understanding who we are in Christ—and how we got there—by grace through faith in Jesus. Pop psychology and positive thinking teach that joy is within you; you just have to think positively to tap into it. But Paul is saying that the source of our joy must be something other than ourselves. In essence, he's saying, "Find your joy exclusively in Jesus."

Rejoicing is not about avoiding difficult circumstances. It is not about avoiding or choosing not to deal with difficulties or challenges. Rather, it's about facing anything and everything that the enemy of God or the world can throw at us, and trusting that because Jesus is living in us and through us, nothing can separate us from God's love, calling, or purposes, and thus we can be content with whatever our portion in life might be.

Paul continues, writing,

"To write the same things to you is no trouble to me and is a safeguard for you. Look out for the dogs, look out for the evildoers, look out for those who mutilate the flesh." *(Philippians 3:1b-2)*

Paul has instructed his readers to rejoice multiple times already in this letter, but it's so important—and so crucial to the growth of our love for Him and for His people—he's saying that it's no trouble for him to write it again. In fact, he'll have more to say about it as we get further into the letter. But he wants us to understand why it's important that we make the choice to rejoice: because it's a safeguard. Our choice to rejoice is a type of protection for us. First, he

142

tells us to look out—to beware—of evildoers who mutilate the flesh.

It might seem that Paul is quickly and abruptly changing the subject here, but we need to see how this is connected to rejoicing in the Lord. What is it that would distract us and divert our attention away from rejoicing in the Lord? Thinking falsely about our relationship with Jesus, for one. There were some false teachers called Judaizers who were going around telling people to look away from the indwelling presence of the Holy Spirit and instructing them to look at the things that were outward—such as circumcision. They were teaching and promoting obedience to the practice of empty, meaningless, surface rituals. Their idea was that anyone who did this was rendered acceptable before God. But these were people who had it all backwards, thinking that if someone acts righteously, THEN that someone is saved, rather than seeing that if someone is saved, THEN they will act righteously. Christianity teaches that we do good works BECAUSE Jesus has saved us; we do not believe that He saves us because we do good works.

Rejoicing in the Lord keeps our focus on Jesus, trusting in His goodness, and that safeguards us from getting the idea that there's any goodness in us apart from Jesus. Rejoicing means finding joy, confidence, and assurance in what Jesus has done, rather than on what we've done. Rejoicing in the Lord reminds us that the work of Jesus was sufficient—it was sufficient to redeem us, to cleanse us, and to allow the Holy Spirit to dwell within us. This is the difference between saying, "Look at what the Lord has done for us" and "Look at what I've done for the Lord!" Paul tells us that those who get this all backwards and thus focus on outward things like rites and rituals as a measure of righteousness are dogs, evildoers, and mutilators (no, please…tell us how you REALLY feel, Paul).

Paul uses something of a play on words here. The Greek word for "mutilate" differs from "circumcision" only in the prefix. The Greek pagans would make cuts and mutilations in their skin as a means of rendering themselves pleasing to God, and the Jews viewed these people as dogs. Paul is saying that these Judaizers teach an equally worthless false religion. So the term "mutilate" refers to the fact that they make marks in the flesh which are void of any real meaning or significance.

Unfortunately, there are still plenty of people who try to make faith necessarily visible and measurable by instituting and embracing man-made rules, who live by a checklist rather than the leading of the Holy Spirit. There are plenty of people who go to church, because it's on the checklist. You have people who participate in Lent, because it's on the checklist. You have people who pray every day, because that's on the checklist. Now, you might be thinking, "What's wrong with going to church or participating in lent, or praying, etc.?" Nothing is wrong with those things, until you're doing those things for the sake of bragging rights. Where do they want the attention to be? On themselves, rather than on the Lord Jesus. This person isn't rejoicing in the Lord; they're rejoicing in what they've done to "prove" their righteousness (which, ironically, hasn't proven their righteousness at all, but has proven their depravity through their adherence to false religion).

Martyn Lloyd-Jones was a magnificent writer and preacher who said, "There are many people who never know the joy of the Lord because they have failed to see themselves as miserable sinners. The only way to be happy in Christ is to be desperately unhappy without Him." See, what happens when your sense of righteousness is based on a checklist of works is that you eventually don't find joy in it anymore; it's never enough.

And yet, this appeals to us so strongly in the flesh, because it's something of an ego boost. At some point in our walk, I am convinced that this is something that we're all tempted (if not persuaded) to do. It's an issue of pride, which every one of us struggles against. We love recognition from others! But the same platform we desire to elevate ourselves upon is also an obstacle of the type of authentic, humble faith that Jesus calls us to. Our works will never be enough to earn us an ounce of righteousness.

Jesus, on the other hand, is enough. There is nothing that you or I can do to become more righteous than He has made us. Our sin was imputed to Him, and His righteousness was transferred to us. That means that we can't make ourselves more righteous, but it also means that we can't make ourselves *less* righteous. That's one of those things that's so amazing and incomprehensible about God's grace!

In comparison to the greatness of God's grace, our works are revealed to be less than amazing, and certainly not incomprehensible.

Look at the contrast that Paul draws for us between those who teach the mutilation of the flesh and thereby practice an artificial faith and those who practice an authentic faith in Jesus.

"For we are the circumcision, who worship by the Spirit of God and glory in Christ Jesus and put no confidence in the flesh." (Philippians 3:3)

Real, authentic faith belongs in Christ alone. It trusts completely in Him and what He did on Calvary. The mature believer knows that they wouldn't last five seconds without Jesus as their source of life before they fell back into sin.

Notice that Paul says that WE are the circumcision. Who is he talking about? He's talking about Christians. He's writing to converted Gentiles and is including them in addition to himself. So he's not talking about his Jewish heritage; he's talking about his (and our) standing in Christ. It had once been that the act of circumcision had set God's people apart from the Gentiles. But in Jesus, anyone who trusts in Him and follows Him is set apart from unbelievers. So circumcision is no longer a mark on one's body—it's a changed heart and nature. Consider what Paul wrote to the Colossians:

"In him also you were circumcised with a circumcision made without hands, by putting off the body of the flesh, by the circumcision of Christ, having been buried with him in baptism, in which you were also raised with him through faith in the powerful working of God, who raised him from the dead." (Colossians 2:11-12)

True believers—those who have trusted fully in the work of Jesus on their behalf—are the circumcision that Paul is talking about. He then goes on to give three characteristics of those who are the true circumcision which demonstrate the authenticity of their faith in Jesus.

First of all, Paul tells us, they worship by the Spirit of God. Worship is an invisible thing that we can't see. It's something that only God can see. Worship isn't the act of singing songs, but it's something that is supposed to be happening inside of us when we sing those songs. See, it's entirely possible to sing all of the right doctrines, and to do so beautifully, and yet be completely lost in sin, because it's just a performance—it's paying lip service to God. The unregenerate heart cannot and will not worship God. But for the authentic believer, the means by which they offer praises to God comes by the indwelling presence of the Holy Spirit. Authentic worship is never about singing on key or saying all of the right things. Authentic worship is what happens when we turn our hearts to God and declare His worth. That, my friends, is how authentic worship is defined. In fact, the very word "worship" is derived from the Old English word, "worthship." When we devote ourselves to His great worth, that's worship. It's not just something that happens in church on Sunday mornings. It's an internal devotion to living outwardly in and for Him.

Secondly, authentic believers glory (or boast) in Christ Jesus. This is in stark contrast to the Judaizers or anyone else who glories in their own works. There are churches out there who give great amounts of money to feed the homeless, and they boast of their generosity. There are churches out there that record and publicize the number of baptisms they have, and they publicly boast about that. In fact, there's a church in Charlotte, North Carolina that has people planted in the church to come forward for baptism as a means of prompting and encouraging others to do the same. It's psychological manipulation! And they boast about it! One of our greatest temptations is to boast or glory in anything else. Authentic faith directs all glory to Christ alone, boasting of nothing but Jesus, and only Jesus.

Third, the authentic believer has no confidence in the flesh. They place no confidence in their works or in any of the things that you can see or measure externally. Their confidence isn't in things that they have done (or in the fact

147

that they've avoided certain sins). Rather, they are confident in Christ's atoning work, realizing that the only reason they can stand before God is because they are in Christ and He is in them. There are people out there who affirm a false doctrine called "sinless perfectionism." That is, they believe that they can reach a point where they are no longer able to sin. That's putting a lot of faith in the flesh, friends. Authentic faith has no such confidence.

Putting all of this into the context of this letter to the Philippians, it's this type of attitude that's required for resolving conflict. One of the wonderful things about the Gospel is that it levels the playing field. Nobody is more qualified than anyone else. Nobody has any right to boast about their titles or their self of personal righteousness, because we all recognize that salvation is not a reward for our righteousness; rather, it's a gift to sinners. You can't earn a gift—all you can do is receive it. Because the playing field is leveled by the Gospel, these two people who are in the midst of the strife in Philippi have no right to pull rank with one another. That type of mindset keeps us humble. Finding our confidence in the Lord and not in the flesh is indeed a humbling reality.

This is all a lesson that Paul had learned as the Holy Spirit gave him perspective on his own life. He knew what it was like to boast in the works of the flesh, and to base his idea of righteousness on the things that were seen externally. We now come to a passage from which we learn a lot about Paul that we may not have gathered elsewhere in Scripture.

"Though I myself have reason for confidence in the flesh also. If anyone else thinks he has reason for confidence in the flesh, I have more: circumcised on the eighth day, of the people of Israel, of the tribe of Benjamin, a Hebrew of Hebrews; as to the law, a Pharisee; as to zeal, a persecutor

of the church; as to righteousness under the law,
blameless." (Philippians 3:4-6)

Paul is saying, "You think you have reason to boast in and have confidence in the flesh? I've got at least one up on you." He goes on to tell us of his ancestry, his orthodoxy, and his external appearance of righteousness. If there was a desired status for Jews, Paul had it. He was a pure Jew—not a convert. He was in the most highly regarded tribe of Israel: the tribe of Benjamin. The tribe of Benjamin had stood by the tribe of Judah when Israel had its civil war, dividing north and south, and dividing the faithless from the faithful. Benjamin was faithful. He was a Pharisee, which means that, unlike the Sadducees, he practiced an orthodox Jewish faith. The Pharisees prided themselves in the fact that they could not only perfectly follow God's laws, but they threw some of their own rules in the mix as well. Oh, and you want to talk about someone who had a zeal for God? Paul had zeal—so much zeal that he persecuted Christians, whom he obviously perceived as a doctrinally-aberrant Jewish cult.

You want to talk about titles? Paul had the highest of them all, as far as his people were concerned. But you know what? We're tempted to get to the point where we feel the same way about ourselves. We're tempted to aim for spiritual titles so that we can get some glory for ourselves. I know and see people who boast of "winning souls." Friends, there is only one soul winner—and He redeemed our souls by shedding His blood for us on Calvary. It honestly breaks my heart when I see and hear people boasting of what they've done, rather than stepping out of the picture completely so that Jesus alone can be glorified. It's all so deceptively tempting for us to want to take the credit for lives being changed!

Paul concludes this section with this radical statement:

"But whatever gain I had, I counted as loss for the sake of Christ." (Philippians 3:7)

All of these titles and accolades had taught Paul one thing: the futility of the flesh. He realized that it was all worthless, because it was all about him. It brought him glory, it gave him boasting rights, it made him feel like he deserved the respect of others. In that sense, the accomplishments and titles he had collected were all gains. But Jesus said, "For what does it profit a man to gain the whole world and forfeit his soul?" (Mark 8:36). What a difficult temptation that is for us, because we're surrounded by people who are trying to gain the world. When I was in seminary, I worked in a bank, and in the entry area of the bank, they would often put advertisements and promotional posters. And there was one in particular which caught my attention. It said, "Why just keep up with the Joneses when you can pass them up?" The promotion was for people to take out a second mortgage on their homes so that they could invest their money in "things"—things that their neighbors would covet; things that their neighbors probably couldn't afford . . . things that would draw them deeper and deeper into debt.

Jesus was reminding us that there are more important things than gaining the world. Because the truth is that we can collect titles and trophies, but none of them come with us to the grave.
Jesus also said, "No one can serve two masters, for either he will hate the one and love the other, or he will be devoted to the one and despise the other" (Matthew 6:24). You cannot rejoice in the flesh and rejoice in the Lord. You cannot be confident in the flesh and in Jesus; it's one or the other. It cannot be both. The principle we learned in

our previous passage was the importance of selflessness. Our passage today is a glimpse of what that principle looks like when it's put into action. It results in us finding our greatest joy in the Lord, rather than in ourselves.

If you're tempted to find ultimate happiness or fulfillment in the things of this world, look to the cross. Look to Calvary. Look at the work that Jesus did on your behalf! If there is anything that you're tempted to do for the sake of maintaining or improving your outward appearance of spirituality, place no confidence in it, but trust fully instead in Jesus. He is enough. His grace is sufficient. When we understand and learn to trust in all that Christ has done for us and continues by the Holy Spirit to do in and through us, we'll learn the same lessons that Paul did.
Accomplishments and titles will come and go, but they're all meaningless in comparison to the eternal life we've been given, which was made possible by the redeeming work of Christ on our behalf. Let that be the basis of our confidence and boasting, in order that Jesus receives all of the glory.

~~~

Chapter 11: "Jesus > Everything"

Philippians 3:8-12

I don't watch a whole lot of television anymore. It used to be that I was able to invest a fair amount of time to a television series, but there was a show from a few years back that changed all of that for me. The name of the show was "Lost." What an appropriate name for a show that ultimately didn't make a whole lot of sense! You might say that I "lost" interest in television after waiting for years to have questions answered in that show, only for everything to end sort of abruptly, with many things left unresolved.

The show was about Oceanic Flight 815, which crashed in the ocean, but close enough to an island that most of the people onboard were able to survive on this island, which turned out to be a very mysterious place. The final season, which was absolutely horrible, had the characters travel to a parallel reality in which the flight never crashed, and we saw how their lives would have gone on through this parallel universe.

The idea of parallel universes isn't unique to Lost, however. Science fiction writers have been writing stories of people traveling to other universes and worlds for centuries. The idea of traveling to a different universe where everything is the exact polar opposite seems to intrigue people. Can you imagine a world in which everything was exactly the opposite as it is now? I would be a fiercely militant atheist, and my atheist friends and acquaintances would love the Lord Jesus as passionately as I do (in this world, of course). And the value system of our culture would be growing in the direction of godliness, forsaking any and every sense of worldliness.

Here's the hook: the world's value system really IS totally opposite of everything that the Gospel stands for. And so when the world looks at us, and when they see the reflection of Biblical values in our lives (as they should), we can expect to be on the receiving end of some serious animosity. It really is like coming from two totally different universes sometimes.

One of the greatest value differences between the world and the Gospel is found in the confidence we place in the flesh. In his letter to the Philippians, Paul made it clear for us that those who live by the values of God will place no confidence in the flesh (3:4). And yet, the world places a tremendous amount of value in the flesh. The values of the Gospel dictate that because our righteousness is based on Christ's righteousness, we have no righteousness of our own to boast of or glory in; rather, we glory in Christ alone. Yet the world is again completely opposite: the world would have a person boast of and glory in their own sense of righteousness, which is based on external, measurable things that they count on to render themselves acceptable to God.

And so what has Paul showed us? In the verses leading up to our passage today, it was like he brought us to his trophy case to show how he might line up according to the world's value system. I used to keep all of these trophies and plaques that I had earned over the years, and so I think of all of those things when I see what Paul is doing. I had plaques for making the Dean's List, trophies for winning karate tournaments and soccer championships, I had a letter inviting me to join a semi-professional soccer team that traveled through Europe. Why did I carry these things around? Because they were once important to me. Similarly, Paul told us that he was a pure-bred Jew (which was a high honor) from the tribe of Benjamin (which was an even greater honor). He told us of how as far as the Law went, he had upheld it perfectly. He's opening up his trophy case and letting us see all of these great accomplishments. But then he says, "But whatever gain I had, I counted as loss for the sake of Christ" (v. 7). This is the equivalent of closing the door to the trophy case, dousing it with gasoline, and setting it all ablaze, as if to say, "If I had to choose between my accomplishments in the flesh and what Christ has accomplished for me, it's a no-brainer because Jesus is the only thing—the only Person—that matters to me."

Paul is now going to give us the one statement that he emphasizes more than anything else that I'm aware of in his writings. He says,

"Indeed, I count everything as loss because of the surpassing worth of knowing Christ Jesus my Lord." (Philippians 3:8a)

In the English translations, we miss how emphatic Paul is here. There's so much emphasis, it's almost comical. He starts off with the word "indeed." But that word is really the translation of five Greek particles all brought together, which is his way of saying, "Don't you dare miss what I'm about to say." As Ray Stedman points out, "What Paul literally is saying is: though, indeed, therefore, at least, even." Why is he doing that? Because he's going to say something that we shouldn't miss. I believe that this is the only time Paul ever does this, so we can be sure that this is supremely important.

So Because Paul has counted as loss all of these accomplishments for the sake of placing his confidence entirely in Christ rather than in himself or his deeds, he says, "I count everything as loss because of the surpassing worth of knowing Christ Jesus my Lord." Paul was willing to give up absolutely everything in order to know and follow Jesus.
Notice with me, if you will, how Paul expands the scope of things he would surrender for Jesus' sake. In verse 7, he refers to "whatever" things he held as a measure of his righteousness. But then here in verse 8, he expands the scope to "everything" and "all things." And we might be tempted to think, "Well, this is Paul, writing in the Bible, so of course he's extreme and radical about his willingness to surrender everything for Jesus. But these days, it's doubtful that anyone else would look at things the same way." But the truth is that Paul isn't just speaking theoretically, and that we find men and women whose greatest desire was to know Jesus scattered across the spectrum of history.

Just this past week, Pastor Mark Driscoll said that he was stepping away from all social media and networking for at least the remainder of the year. Why? Ultimately, to grow in his relationship with Jesus.

C.S. Lewis was denied a professorship at Oxford University. Why? Because the university had felt embarrassed that Lewis had written "Mere Christianity," one of the greatest theological books of the last century. What teaching position could be more coveted than that? And yet Lewis abandoned his pursuit of it for the sake of knowing Jesus.

In 1536, William Tyndale was put to death as a martyr for making Bibles available in what was at the time the modern vernacular. He was willing to give his life to know Jesus and to make Christ known.

John Huss was martyred in 1415 for standing against the Roman Catholic Church on doctrines. Ultimately, it was his death that helped to birth the Reformation, but knowing Jesus cost him anything and everything that he held dear, including his life.

Augustine wrote this in his confessions: "But where in all that long time was my free will, and from what deep sunken hiding-place was it suddenly summoned forth in the moment in which I bowed my neck to Your easy yoke and my shoulders to Your light burden, Christ Jesus, my Helper and Redeemer? How lovely I suddenly found it to be free from the loveliness of those vanities, so that now it was a joy to renounce what I had been so afraid to lose. For You cast them out of me, O true and supreme Loveliness, You cast them out of me and took their place in me, You who are sweeter than all pleasure."

In the lives and in the written words of uncountable Christians throughout history, you see a major theme emerge: knowing and being known by Jesus is better than anything that this world has to offer.

This should cause us to think. This should cause us to reflect. We're forced to ask ourselves, "What have I freely surrendered for the sake of knowing Jesus? What would I surrender to know Him more fully and deeply?" Or maybe we should ask, conversely, "What would I NOT surrender for the sake of Jesus?" What about your car? What about your bank account, or your house, or your 401k, or your ability to be recognized and liked? What about your family? Do you realize that that's what so many Muslims around the world have to do when they convert to Christianity? They often essentially have to count their family as loss for the sake of knowing Jesus Christ. What about your life? Could you give that up, if you had to pick and choose?

The question really boils down to two questions: 1) what is the basis of your standing before God? Is it Jesus or is it something you've done or regularly do? 2) Is knowing and being known by Jesus your greatest desire? You don't need to share your real thoughts and feelings about that question with me or anyone else, but your answer WILL be revealed when you stand before the Lord Jesus someday. In a country that is filled with cultural, carnally-minded Christians who know very little of sacrifice, persecution, and tribulation, this is an important question, because there will be people who have never had this question cross their minds, and someday when they stand before Jesus, He's going to say to them, "I never knew you. Depart from Me, you workers of lawlessness" (Matt. 7:23). And I can only imagine that as they're being dragged away from His presence to the depths of hell, they'll be saying, "Wait! Look at all of these things I did—I tithed gross, not net! My great grandfather helped plant a church! I went to church almost every Christmas and Easter! I never invited my friends, but I didn't want to make You seem offensive to people!"

What a horrible day that will be for some people, when Jesus says, "Your trophy case of titles and deeds in the flesh doesn't mean anything to Me."

Now, don't get me wrong. I want you to understand that this is of paramount importance for the Christian, but I also understand that we're all in the process of learning how to make this even more of a reality in our lives. I don't think that it's very likely that Paul suddenly gained this perspective on the road to Damascus, where he was converted. See, our conversion is in one sense the end of something (it's the end of our life without Christ), but in another sense, it's the beginning of this process called sanctification. Our conversion is the end of one road, but the beginning of another. After Paul was converted, he spent years in Arabia, according to what Paul says in Galatians 1:17. It was only after many years of reflecting and growing in the Lord Jesus that he was able to truly understand that nothing was more important in life than knowing and being known by the Lord Jesus.

The Lord knew how to bring Paul to the place where he saw the worthlessness of everything that this world has to offer. Notice the change in tense between verses 7 and 8? First Paul said, "I *counted* as loss," but now he says, "I count." In other words, he made a decision, and to this day, he stands by it. As he writes this, he was reaffirming his choice daily, and he's implicitly challenging us as his readers to do the same thing.

The more fully we release the things we hold dear in the flesh or in this world, the more clearly we see what Paul saw: the surpassing worth of knowing Jesus. The more we know Jesus, the more He changes the way we value everything.

There one more thing I want us to see before we continue, and that is a parallel that Paul has slipped in here, very subtly.

"[Jesus] did not <u>count</u> equality with God a thing to be grasped . . ." (2:6)

158

"I count everything as loss . . ." (3:8)

Well played, Paul . . . well played. You might say that Paul didn't count the accomplishments of the flesh—or anything else for that matter—a thing to be grasped in comparison to the greatness of knowing and being known by Jesus.

"For His sake I have suffered the loss of all things and count them as rubbish, in order that I may gain Christ" (Philippians 3:8b)

We might wonder if Paul ever missed the days when he had all of these accomplishments and statuses in the flesh which he could boast about, but he leaves no doubt in anyone's mind here, saying that everything else is "rubbish" in comparison to gaining Christ. The word "rubbish" is probably far too clean to translate exactly what Paul is saying here. This is the only place in the whole New Testament that this term is used. One commentator notes that "in some Greek texts this term refers 'specifically to human excrement'" (Hansen, p. 236). This is actually a kind of vulgar term, but again, we have to understand that Paul is making what is possibly the most emphatic statement he ever makes in his letters. But the point is clear: because Jesus is far more valuable and far more worthy than anything that this world has to offer, we need to learn to see anything that stands in the way of us wholeheartedly pursuing Jesus as vulgar, offensive, and repulsive. What do we do with human excrement? We get rid of it, right? So what do you think we should do when we see that something is getting in the way of us pursuing Jesus wholeheartedly? The truth is that sometimes our lives need a royal flush, and I'm not talking about a hand in poker!

It is entirely possible for a Christian to never fully understand what it means to "gain Christ" in the sense that Paul is using here. Why? Because we so often don't see certain things in our lives for the "rubbish" that they are. We don't see that certain things that might hinder our walk with Jesus pale in comparison to knowing and being known by Him. But as Jesus said, "Nobody can serve two masters." The only reason that's challenging for us is because we so often have this belief that we can pursue Jesus AND all of these other things wholeheartedly. But the truth is that we can't.

What's kind of ironic here is that Paul isn't talking about things that are inherently wicked; he's talking about things that, in accordance with the flesh, are typically perceived as good or even outstanding. That's what makes these things so deeply deceptive, and thus they don't deserve our confidence or our devotion. The more we let go of everything else (in the sense that we hold it with an open hand, as good stewards, rather than with a clenched fist), the more of Christ we will gain. This means changing our values, doing a 180-degree turn around from the ways of the world. It means going against the flow. No wonder the world thinks we're crazy sometimes! And yet, when we forsake everything, counting it as garbage in comparison to gaining Christ, we see that there are at least three ways in which we "gain Christ."

"and be found in Him, not having a righteousness of my own that comes from the law, but that which comes through faith in Christ, the righteousness from God that depends on faith;" (Philippians 3:9)

Paul says that when we gain Christ, we're found in Him. That means that we're covered by His righteousness, because He's in us, and we're in Him. His righteousness

160

has been imputed to us, and every last one of our sins was transferred to Him. The point that he's making is that we can trust in Christ's righteousness, but we can't trust in our own. And that's why I don't believe that a person can lose their salvation—because it's not based on our faithfulness; it's based on His! If a person *could* lose their salvation, they would. Every one of us would fall away, because our greatest righteousness is like a filthy rag before God. He doesn't want it!

See, the Judaizers had a righteousness, but theirs was a righteousness on the surface that comes from the Law, which is diametrically opposed to the righteousness that comes through faith in Christ. The righteousness of man depends on that person's ability to uphold God's standard, but Paul had learned that no matter how good a person is at keeping the Law (which Paul himself could do better than most), and no matter how much self-improvement a person has gone through, or how much effort a person is able to put forth, it was never enough. It might look good before people, because people only see what's on the surface, but God rejects it.

The author of Hebrews (probably Paul) said that "without faith it is impossible to please Him" (11:6). The implication there is pretty clear: our own sense of righteousness does not please Him. True righteousness is a gift from God—it's not something that we can be good enough on our own to claim. That's why we say that we're saved by grace alone through faith alone.

First and foremost, to gain Christ means to be found in Him, having the righteousness that He transferred to us on the Cross.

Secondly, to "gain Christ" means . . .

"that I may know Him and the power of His resurrection, and may share His sufferings, becoming like Him in His death" (Philippians 3:10)

The world is filled with people who know *about* Christ, but Paul is saying that by gaining Christ, we don't just know *about* Him; rather, we know Him. This is the goal of every step in our faith journeys: to gain Christ, to be found in Him, and to know Him. And that's made possible by the power of His resurrection. What does it mean to know the power of His resurrection? I think we find a clue in Romans 8:11, where we read, "If the Spirit of Him who raised Jesus from the dead dwells in you, He who raised Christ Jesus from the dead will also give life to your mortal bodies through His Spirit who dwells in you." Paul is talking about knowing the power of the Holy Spirit dwelling within us. We receive what's referred to as the "baptism of the Holy Spirit" upon conversion, but to actually know that power (in the experiential sense) requires a growing process.

What was Paul's goal before his conversion to Christianity? To uphold the Law of Moses flawlessly. But that's contrasted with his goal as a Christian, which is knowing Jesus. This is the end goal toward which we must all strive: to relationally and experientially know Jesus more and more deeply, and more and more intimately. And what Paul does here is link two things together that are inseparable to knowing Christ. If you know Christ, you will experience the power of His resurrection (the Holy Spirit), which will strengthen and will lead us to share in His sufferings.

The Christian life becomes much more complicated than it needs to be when we don't understand that we will share in

His sufferings. Jesus could have lived a full life and died of old age . . . if He had chosen not to suffer. But the reality is that there will be consequences for taking a stand for the righteousness of Christ. Jesus said that if we want to follow Him, we must deny ourselves (Mark 8:34). Don't think for a second that you can do that without suffering in some way. Paul told the Romans, "For if you live according to the flesh you will die, but if by the Spirit you put to death the deeds of the body, you will live" (8:13). Don't think for a second that you can do that without suffering in some way.

You see, the world will look at us and say, "You're depriving yourself of so much pleasure!" And we'll be tempted (if not enticed) to believe them! Why? Because the flesh is so easily deceived. I look at someone like Tim Tebow (who actually did have a winning record in the NFL), and all of the harassment he went through for his faith. Someone might say to him, "You know, Tim, you might still be in the NFL if you'd just keep your faith private." And knowing what I know about Tim Tebow, he'd say "I consider the NFL to be rubbish in comparison to gaining Christ, being found in Christ, and knowing Christ, sharing in His sufferings."

Under the Law, animals were put to death as sacrifices. But under the New Covenant, God no longer wants us to make sacrifices—He wants us to BE sacrifices: living sacrifices. Because to obey is greater than sacrifice (1st Samuel 15:22).

Knowing (in the experiential sense) the power of His resurrection is what gives us the strength and the determination to participate in the sufferings of Jesus. This power is sufficient to see us through the deepest valleys that life has to offer, and it's sufficient to strengthen us

163

when the world throws its best shot in our direction. It's what turns mourning into gladness, and turns despair to hope. It's in that process of learning how to experience resurrection power in our lives that we grow in our relationship with Jesus, where we learn to know Him on a deeper level.

Paul tells us that by doing this, we become like Jesus in His death. That is something of a confusing statement if we don't consider what Paul has already told us about the death of Jesus. Remember that back in chapter two, Paul told us that Jesus "humbled himself by becoming obedient to the point of death" (v. 8). So when Paul talks about becoming like Christ in His death, he means that he's learning to humble himself by becoming obedient to the will of God. The truth is—and we all know it—that we don't become obedient to God the moment that we are regenerated. A person who is not born again can't be obedient to God, and when we're born again, it's not like we automatically start being obedient. It simply means that it's suddenly an option to us. But we don't automatically or instinctively or consistently exercise that option the from the moment we're converted. That's like expecting a new born baby to pick himself right up and walk out of the hospital! It's a ridiculous thought, right? Because we understand that there's a process of growing and learning that comes before walking. The same is true of learning to humble ourselves in obedience to the will of God. That's undoubtedly one of the reasons why, when Paul was giving Timothy instructions about the qualifications of a pastor, he says, "He must not be a recent convert" (1st Timothy 3:6).

The first reason to wholeheartedly pursue and gain Christ is that we may be found in Him, that, secondly, we may know Him, and third,

"that perhaps I may attain the resurrection from the dead."
(Philippians 3:11)

If the whole aim of each and every step of the Christian life is to gain Christ, and therefore to be found in Him and to know Him, the journey concludes here. The journey of faith lasts from regeneration until resurrection. It's because of this great hope that Paul knows that death doesn't get the final word. And so Paul can go through the valleys and the trials and the sufferings of life without having his faith shaken—but strengthened!—because if death has lost its hold on his life, then what was there to hold him back and separate him from God's love?

Now, someone might read this and think that Paul sounds somewhat uncertain, since he sounds like he might be doubting this, based on the way he uses the word "somehow." But he's not uncertain at all. Rather, we need to understand that his hope was to experience the Second Coming of Christ in his lifetime. But as he wrote this, he knew that there was a real possibility of him being killed. If that was to be the case, then he would experience the resurrection from the dead.

Either way, Paul knew that he was safe in his position in Jesus, and that Jesus was going to bring Paul to Himself one day, and nothing could stand in the way of that becoming a reality. That's why he wrote to the Romans,

"And those whom He predestined He also called, and those whom He called He also justified, and those whom He justified he also glorified." (Romans 8:30)

It's the day of glorification that Paul has in mind. He knows that because he's been justified by faith, he will experience this day of glorification, when we see Jesus face to face as He really is, and then become like Him.

Paul's desire is for his readers to know that there is no power on earth and no earthly thing that compares to Jesus. Jesus is infinitely more worthy than the greatest earthly treasures.

I used to regularly go fishing in central Nevada. We would use salmon eggs to catch rainbow trout, but there were German brown trout in this lake as well. Of course, German browns are significantly larger than stock-size rainbow trout. And so one time, I saw this enormous German brown trout swimming about ten feet out from the shore. I baited my line with salmon eggs and threw my line right in front of this fish. This was when I learned that German browns aren't even a little bit interested in salmon eggs. It wasn't even tempting for him. As far as he was concerned, my bait was just a piece of trash floating in the lake.

The challenge that Paul is giving us here is to view anything in life that might stand in the way of our pursuing Christ the same way—as trash, or as something to be eliminated from our path. Our job is to learn what it means to humble ourselves and be obedient to the will of God by the leading and empowerment of the Holy Spirit. He'll give us the strength and the wisdom to recognize when the enemy is trying to lure us toward something other than Jesus, if we'll just listen to Him. When temptation splashes down right in front of you, see it for what it is: compared to gaining Christ, everything else is worthless rubbish. Pursuing Christ more and more wholeheartedly is not just our top priority—it's everything; it's what the Christian life is all about. And the more we do it, the more we grow in

Him and the more deeply we know Him and see His all-surpassing worth.

~~~

Chapter 12: Pressing On, Striving Forward

Philippians 3:12-16

Life is filled with boundaries and things that are best left alone. Yet, I'm one of those people who didn't always take what I was told and warned about at face value. Even as a child, I was always the one who had to figure things out the hard way, which usually involved me not listening to the warnings my parents would give me, and just figuring out through my own experience that my parents were right all along.

These days, we're doing a lot to warn our kids about what they post to their Facebook and Twitter accounts, because we know that once something is on the internet, there's no way to control whose hands it falls into, where it might end up, or how it might come back to bite them. But does that stop them? Unfortunately, a lot of the time, it does not.

It was Helen Keller who once said, "Life is a succession of lessons which must be lived to be understood." Indeed, as we grow older, we grow wiser, and we start to see lessons in many aspects of life that we had maybe never considered before. As we continue with our study of the book of Philippians, we're going to see that, like Helen Keller, Paul viewed life as a succession of lessons.

It is a wonderful thing to realize that God deals with each of us individually, because we're all unique (just like everyone else, right?). We go through this journey of growing in Christ's likeness, but each of us faces different obstacles, different temptations, and different trials along the way. We will all have our moments of failure as well. I certainly have mine, and you certainly have yours. But the more life experience we have with these moments of failure, the more we must come to see those moments as valuable life lessons. If nothing else, those moments of failure teach us not to put any confidence in the flesh, as Paul instructed us back in verse 3 of this the third chapter of Philippians.

This is where it becomes so important to realize that salvation comes in stages. We get confused and discouraged when we don't keep in mind that justification isn't the same as sanctification. Justification is when we're once and for all declared not guilty by God's grace alone through faith alone in Christ alone. Justification is when we're freed from the penalty of sin, and is instantaneous. Sanctification is the process in which we're freed from the power and influence of sin. It's in this process that the Holy Spirit works in us and through us to teach us to walk in accordance with the will of God. Our salvation will be complete when we experience glorification: the moment when we enter into eternity in the presence of God, forever removed from the presence of sin.

In the meantime—until that glorious day—we will all make mistakes and we will all sin from time to time. And this is where we realize how glorious and majestic the grace of God truly is. The question is: will your failures define and anchor your identity?

Paul has told us that he has surrendered everything, counting it worthless in comparison to knowing Jesus. He told us that he suffered the loss of all things in order that he could gain Christ, in order that he could be found in Christ, in order that he could know Christ and the power of the resurrection, and in order that he could experience the resurrection of the dead one day. But we saw that this wasn't the attitude that Paul had from the moment he converted to Christianity. Rather, he had learned over time to pursue Jesus wholeheartedly. It was one of those lessons that could only be learned through life experience. He was a work in progress. Consider what he writes as he continues:

"Not that I have already obtained this or am already perfect, but I press on to make it my own, because Christ Jesus has made me His own." (Philippians 3:12)

What a comfort that should be to us in those moments of failure! We are all like clay in the hands of the Potter, who is working out our flaws and defects as only He can . . . but as long as we're still living, He's still working on us! Despite his incredible passion for pursuing Jesus full speed ahead, Paul is acknowledging that he still has struggles, he still has moments of failure, he still makes a mess of things sometimes, and yet he still has the confidence and the assurance of belonging to Jesus. The truth is that no matter how passionate we are about Jesus, and no matter how wholeheartedly we are committed to pursuing him, our passionate intentions do not render us perfect.

It goes without saying that this is a major contrast when you compare this sentiment with the opinion that he once had about himself in the flesh. He told us back in verse 6 that, as far as the Law goes, he was perfect ("blameless" was the word he used). But here he is, confessing that he's not. This is one of the great works of the Holy Spirit in our lives—He makes us aware of how far we are from the goal, and He gives us the strength to continue making progress. See, the more mature a Christian is, the more aware they are of their faults and failures. But the mature Christian will know that he nevertheless belongs to Jesus, because Jesus has made him His own.

What I'm going to start out by challenging you to do today is to see your faults and failures in light of this verse. There are right ways and wrong ways to deal with our struggles. One of the worst things a person can do is refuse to acknowledge the fact that the struggle even exists within them. But it's just as bad, if not worse, to acknowledge the struggle, and to allow it to keep you anchored down in your past failures.

See, the truth is that we all have "buts." Let me explain. Maybe you feel like God would have you serve Him in a certain way, and maybe you want to, but . . . you don't think you're ready. Or you think, "I would, BUT I've messed up so badly in the past." You might say that the central message of our passage today is to get rid of your "buts"!

It's also wrong to try to tackle the struggle by ourselves, as if we're able to overcome it on our own strength. Do not place that much confidence in the flesh!

The right way to face our struggles is to look to Jesus, and to see ourselves—warts, failures and all—in light of the fact that Jesus has already made us His own, and to press on. The work of redemption was done by Him. We come into this life as weak, broken people, and even after we come to Jesus, we experience the reality of weakness and brokenness in our lives. The process of sanctification in

171

which we're freed from the power of sin does not come by practicing moralism and it does not come through behavior modification. It comes by looking to and pursuing Jesus more and more, pressing on in our wholehearted pursuit of Him.

Paul wrote to the Corinthians:

"And we all . . . are being transformed into the same image from one degree of glory to another." (2nd Corinthians 3:18)

What Paul is saying here is that all of the redeemed are being transformed into the image of Christ, no matter where we are in that process. If you think of it in terms of an elevator inside of a skyscraper, I think this will make perfect sense. When you walk into the lobby area of the Empire State Building, you'll find several elevators on the bottom floor. Imagine that that represents the moment you first trusted in Christ and repented, and were therefore in Christ. In fact, the Empire State Building has a total of 73 elevators, so when you get into an elevator, you can be sure that there are some people who are closer to the top than you are. But you're all heading to the same place, no matter how high up you might be at any given moment.

The reason we continue to pursue Jesus above all things, pressing on despite our failures, is because He always has more than enough grace to see us through even our deepest faults and failures. His mercies are new every morning. He is more than sufficient to bring us through every situation and ultimately bring us to Himself, because He has already made us His own.

It's in this process of pressing on that we realize that this truly is a relationship that we have with Jesus. A relationship requires two people who are actively engaged in building a bond between them. In our walk with Jesus, He took the initiative, making us His own, and we press on, pursuing Him with more and more determination.

So press on—and continue to press on—and don't allow yourself to be held back by guilt, apathy, or complacency. And do not let the reality of your imperfections discourage you. Rather, continue taking steps to know and grow in Jesus. The decision to count everything as rubbish in comparison to gaining Christ was only the beginning of what must be a daily commitment to press on and pursue Jesus above everything else. This is what the whole Christian life is all about. It's in this process that we're sanctified and grow in Christ's likeness, and it's in this process that we find that only Jesus truly satisfies. And because Jesus is the only source of true satisfaction, only He is worthy of our wholehearted pursuit.

And just for good measure, Paul continues with this train of thought, telling us what it will take for us to successfully press on. And so he writes:

"Brothers, I do not consider that I have made it my own. But one thing I do: forgetting what lies behind and straining forward to what lies ahead, I press on toward the goal for the prize of the upward call of God in Christ Jesus." (Philippians 3:13-14)

As Paul writes this, it's almost like he's aware of the fact that some might not believe that he's not perfect, and so he reiterates it, as if to look us in the eye and say, "No, I'm sincere. I know that I am not anywhere near perfect." But he's not letting that hold him back from pressing on!

Notice the parallel between verses 11 and 12. In verse 11, he says "Christ Jesus has made me His own." Here in verse

12, he says of his imperfections, "I do not consider that I have made it my own."

The key to pressing on and growing closer to Jesus is forgetting what lies behind. This is probably a good time to make a clarification, because sometimes it's good to remember, and sometimes it's bad. Sometimes God wants us to remember, and sometimes He doesn't. For example, God told the Israelites to celebrate the Passover every year so that they would remember the way that God had delivered them from slavery. And yet, here in this passage, Paul is saying forget the past. What makes the difference between things we should remember and things we should forget? In a nutshell, I think the answer is as simple as saying that we should remember the things that draw us closer to God. We should forget the things that unnecessarily make us feel shame and which draw us back to the past, thereby stifling our growth.

With this in mind, we have to understand that the key to pressing on and growing closer to Jesus is forgetting things from the past that anchor us and weigh us down in the sense that we release the lingering guilt and shame they may cause in us. It means letting go of the faults, the shortcomings, the moral failures. This is a place where we need to understand the difference between guilt and shame. We feel guilt when we do something bad. Paul has already revealed that he's less than perfect, which means that he still does bad things sometimes. But Christianity has an answer for that—our debt was paid in full in the atoning death of Jesus, and thus our guilt doesn't remain. The guilt for our sin was cast onto Jesus, and He took it so far away, we can never take ownership of it again. As the psalmist wrote, "As far as the east is from the west, so far He removed our transgressions from us" (Psalm 103:12).

So what keeps us from moving forward? A sense of shame. Guilt is when we do something bad. Shame is when we feel like our badness defines us, and thus we are bad. But when we look to the cross, we see the love of a Savior named Jesus whose righteousness was imputed to us. It's the righteousness of Christ that defines us now—it's not just central to our identity, it IS our identity. There's no place in the life of the Christian for lingering shame.

Let's say that you had a backpack that you wore everywhere you went, and every time you fell short, you had to put a 5-pound weight in there. How long would it be before you were absolutely crushed by that backpack? There are days when I'd be lucky to last ten minutes, and I'm a pretty strong guy! By God's grace, Jesus invites us to drop the backpack, because it will slow us down—if not prevent us entirely—from pursuing Jesus with all of our heart, soul, mind, and strength.

That's why David wrote, "Wash me, and I shall be whiter than snow" (Psalm. 51:7). We've all heard the song: "Jesus paid it all. All to Him, I owe. Sin had left a crimson stain, He washed it white as snow." The truth is, we're whiter than snow. Jesus has rendered us more cleansed and more pure than we could possibly know.

The fact that we're able to dwell on memories and experience a sense of prolonged shame is one of those things that sets us apart from the animal kingdom. Animals don't remember countless events in their lives, and the only time they experience emotion is when something related to an action has trained them to feel things like fear or happiness. Human beings, on the other hand, can dwell on mistakes and failures all day long—for months! Or years!

Think about this from Paul's perspective: he had persecuted the people that Jesus died to redeem, and thus considered himself the chief of sinners. The fact that he was responsible for the death and persecution of Christians very easily could have stuck with him and haunted him for the rest of his life, but only if he allowed it to!

Like Paul, there are some moments in my lifetime that I could look back on and think about what a jerk I was. I've made some mistakes in my life that make me cringe when I think about them. But those things don't define who I am anymore. The real question is this: would I do the same thing today if I was in able to do it again? Absolutely not!

And the same principle goes for each of us. We learn from the past, but we have to live in the present. The burden of the past can be spiritually-paralyzing, if we're not careful. So release the guilt and shame you feel the mistakes you've made past! Would you do things differently today? Hebrews 4:16 instructs us, "Let us then approach the throne of grace with confidence, so that we may receive mercy and find grace to help us in our time of need." It's pretty difficult, if not impossible, to approach the throne of grace with confidence when we're feeling bound by guilt and shame.

See, if there's one thing that's just as bad as sinning, it's refusing to release our sense of guilt and shame, and thus missing opportunities that God is placing before us now. Now, I'm not trying to sound like Dr. Phil or some pop-psychology nut, but there comes a time when we really do have to forgive ourselves and release our sense of guilt and shame. C.S. Lewis put it this way: "I think that if God forgives us we must forgive ourselves. Otherwise, it is almost like setting up ourselves as a higher tribunal than Him." If God forgives us, who are we to say, "Well, you might forgive me, God, but I demand penance and have higher demands before I let this one go." And this is a serious struggle for some people. It keeps some people anchored to their past, and it causes them to miss the opportunities that God is giving them in the present!

Several years ago now, there was a commercial by Nike in which an athlete says, "I've missed more than 9,000 shots in my career. I've lost almost 300 games. Twenty-six times, I was trusted to take the game-winning shot and missed. I've failed over and over and over again in my life, and that is why I succeed." Of course, if you remember that commercial, you know that those words were spoken by Michael Jordan, who is hands-down the greatest basketball player to ever play the game. I remember watching Jordan often when he was an active player. We all remember when he retired for a while, due to the death of his father. But did you watch the game against the Indianapolis Pacers when he came back? He started out by missing at least five or ten shots. But don't think for one second that he stopped shooting just because he was missing. He wasn't dwelling on the missed shots—he was moving forward, doing what he knew how to do.

Every one of us has done things that we might be tempted to feel shame for, and every one of us has to live in the tension of who or what we want to be and who we really are. And so we can learn from the past, but we must live in the present, as we look to the future. We all have to intentionally prevent the past from being an obstacle to the future. That means being aware of who we are now, but also being aware of who we want to be, and pressing on, straining forward to the goal.

I love that Paul uses a metaphor as a race here: he's pressing toward the goal for the prize. With the imagery that Paul is giving, I'm reminded of a racing lesson from the movie *Chariots of Fire*: don't look back—it slows you down! When we forget the past, it gives us the freedom to strive toward the future, with the pursuit of Jesus as the one thing we're focused on doing. That's the prize—a closer sense of fellowship and union with Jesus is the prize.

Think of it this way: what is the reward for having a good, long-lasting, healthy marriage? That in itself is the reward. It's the same with Jesus; we pursue a closer walk with Him and a deeper love for Him because a closer walk with Him and a deeper love for Him are the most rewarding things that exist!

Let's remember that Paul was writing to a church that was on the verge of division, and Paul was well aware of the fact that both of the feuding leaders in the Philippian church would be considered, for all intents and purposes, to be mature believers. And so now he's going to throw down the gauntlet, challenging them to put this principle of pressing on in the pursuit of Christ into action.

"Let those of us who are mature think this way, and if in anything you think otherwise, God will reveal that also to you. Only let us hold true to what we have attained."
(Philippians 3:15-16)

It's very interesting that Paul refers to himself as mature here. The Greek root word that gets translated as "mature" is the same root word for "perfect." Paul has insisted that he's not perfect, but this creates what might appear to be a contradiction. But we need to understand that he's turned the entire concept of perfectionism upside down. What we see then is that Christian maturity is demonstrated in something of a paradox: that is, it takes some serious

178

maturity to realize that we're NOT perfect, and to nevertheless continue pursuing Christ wholeheartedly.

What Paul is doing here is encouraging his readers to put his exhortation to be like-minded into action (cf., 2:2). This requires a steadfast commitment to radical humility.

But notice what Paul says next. He says, "And if in anything you think otherwise, God will reveal that also to you." What an amazing sense of confidence Paul had in the ongoing work of the Holy Spirit in the lives of his fellow Christians! Paul isn't asking them to take his word for it, just because he's Paul and he said so. He knows that they might not agree with him, but he leaves any remaining convincing that they may have needed in God's hands. He knew that God would reveal the truth to them if they would simply keep themselves humble enough to have an open mind about it.

Paul concludes this passage by instructing his readers to "hold true to what we have attained." The term "hold true" literally means "to stay in line." It's a military term. If you've ever watched a military march, it's amazing to watch how perfectly lined up they are with one another! That's essentially what Paul is encouraging them to do, in a sense. What would you think of a military line-up in which everyone was standing wherever they wanted to stand— some slouching over, some standing up right, some watching the butterflies fluttering over in the bushes? Rather than everyone marching to the beat of their own drummer and doing their own thing, Paul is instructing them to remain in formation! In other words, "Stick together, and see one another through the challenges that you're facing."

We are all in different stages of pursuing Christ. Some of you may have just recently begun. Some of you have been pursuing Christ for more than 50 years. And every one of us has the same orders: be faithful to what you know, and continue to grow in your learning about and striving toward Jesus. The fact that we lack perfect and complete knowledge isn't an excuse for not putting what we do know into action.

When Jonathan Edwards, the great Reformed preacher from the 1700's, was 17 years old, he sat down and wrote out 21 resolutions that he had for his life. He would constantly revisit this list, and added resolutions as he saw that they were necessary. By the time he died, he had written out a total of 70 resolutions. Not only that, but it seems that he may have prioritized them, as well, because the number one resolution at the top of the list said this: "Being sensible that I am unable to do anything without God's help, I do humbly entreat Him by His grace to enable me to keep these resolutions.... Remember to read over these Resolutions once a week."

Throughout his life, he did weekly "self-checks," and he would regularly record his progress and areas in which he sought further help from the Lord.

Each of us is a work in progress. We're like clay in the hands of a Potter who knows and loves His work. We are all on this journey of learning to become more and more like Jesus. That's the goal that we're all running toward. If you have grown tired, I encourage you to press on and strive forward to the future, taking steps to grow closer to Jesus. Maybe that means journaling like Jonathan Edwards did. Maybe it means joining one of our small groups. Maybe it means pressing forward by intentionally learning to leave your baggage from the past right there—in the past. Wherever you may be on this journey called "sanctification," know that the reward of pursuing Christ gets sweeter and sweeter, the longer you do it. I sometimes tell my wife, "I can't wait to get old with you." And I can't wait to look back on 50, 60, or maybe even 70 years of pursuing Jesus someday (Lord willing!). His grace has blotted out our mistakes and has given us the freedom to pursue Him with reckless abandon. Only God's amazing grace can free us to truly learn from the past without lingering in the past, and to live in the present while looking to a future of eternal bliss in the presence of the Savior!

~~~

Chapter 13: Not of this World

Philippians 3:17-21

There's a story of brother and his younger sister who were playing church together, while their parents listened in from the other room. The little boy preached a mini-sermon on David and Goliath and his younger sister listened. At the end of the sermon, the boy prayed and ended his prayer with the words, "In the name of the Father, Son, and Holy Spirit." The little girl chimed in, adding, "And to the republic for which it stands."

While this is a cute story, it illustrates an issue that every Christian must come to terms with: the issue of dual citizenship. It's easy to say, "This world is not my home. I'm just passing through." But to live like we actually believe that is quite challenging, and to give our allegiance first and foremost to the Kingdom of Heaven takes some intentionality. There are scores of church-goers in our country who believe that to be American is to be a Christian, but that has never truly been the case. Rather, Christians, while living in this world, are referred to in Scripture as "aliens." That's why Peter wrote, "Beloved, I urge you as *aliens* and strangers to abstain from fleshly lusts which wage war against the soul" (1st Peter 2:11).

Having listed off a few examples of faithful people in the Scriptures who had lived as exiles and aliens on earth, the author of Hebrews says, "All these died in faith, without receiving the promises, but having seen them and having welcomed them from a distance, and having confessed that they were strangers and exiles on the earth" (Hebrews 11:13). He concludes his discussion of their dual citizenship, writing, "They desire a better *country,* that is, a heavenly one. Therefore God is not ashamed to be called their God; for He has prepared a city for them" (v. 16).

Dual citizenship was a concept that the Philippians undoubtedly could relate to, considering that they were located in Macedonia, and yet were still a colony of the Roman Empire. For that reason, Paul will use this as a metaphor for their situation as a means of showing teaching some very important principles for living out our Christian faith in the here and now, as we live on earth as citizens of Heaven.

Paul has been explaining the importance of pursuing Jesus and growing in the likeness of Jesus, even though he knows that it's a process that won't be completed in this lifetime. Nevertheless, Paul knew that maturity in the Christian life was something of a paradox in that it is demonstrated in one's ability to identify their shortcomings and imperfections, and to continue pursuing the goal of Christlikeness despite our weakness. In the previous passage we looked at, Paul told us that we must forget those moments of failure in our past and press on, like a long-distance runner who strives for the goal, and doesn't look back over his shoulder.

Paul was writing to a church that is just like any other church: it was led by fallible people who had weaknesses and short-comings just like anyone else. And he knew that if the two leaders who were in the middle of the strife that was growing in the church would simply humble themselves, recognize their failures, and move forward with the resolution to never part ways, the strife and division would cease. One of the major reasons that churches experience strife and division is because people get too focused on this world, and lose sight of the fact that we are first and foremost to live as citizens of God's Kingdom. When we lose sight of that reality, conflict goes unresolved, often because people are too busy jockeying for power.

This has always been a very real sickness in the church. In the passage at hand, Paul is going to give us some principles which can help to keep these types of problems at bay. Paul continues, writing:

"Brothers, join in imitating me, and keep your eyes on those who walk according to the example you have in us." (Philippians 3:17)

I recently saw a Christian t-shirt that expressed the sentiment that Christians shouldn't imitate anyone but Jesus. In light of verses like this one, I can't say that that's exactly true. In his first letter to the Corinthian church, Paul urged them to imitate him, writing, "Be imitators of me, as I am of Christ" (1 Cor. 11:1). In Hebrews, we're instructed to be "imitators of those who through faith and patience inherit the promises" (Hebrews 12:6).

See, there is a time to imitate people, and there's a time to not imitate people. The distinction is actually pretty simple: it's a good thing to imitate other mature Christians insofar as they demonstrate Christlike character, but we don't want to imitate others in areas where they don't demonstrate Christlike character. That is such an important distinction, because there is a tendency for all of us to imitate those we admire. That's why our kids instinctively imitate what they see on television! That's why our teens

184

imitate pop stars or Hollywood stars. We need to turn their eyes and minds to Christian role-models.

For me, I look at guys like Francis Chan and Paul Washer, and I there's a part of me that naturally wants to imitate them because their passion for Jesus and for teaching the Gospel is absolutely insane! And when I listen to them or read their books, I catch myself thinking to myself, "Wow . . . I sure wish I could express that much passion for Jesus!" I've been reading a biography about John Calvin, which has taught me about how devoted he was to Jesus, and how much time he put into his studying, and again—I find that his passion for Jesus was contagious!

One of the best things we can do if we want to grow in our walk with Jesus is to have a mentor or a guide. That's part of the discipleship process. People don't become disciples by default—they have to be made. They have to be taught, and some things are caught, not taught. That's one place where healthy imitation comes into play.

So the first principle that Paul gives us here is that mature Christians make ideal role-models for other Christians. We must keep in mind that they are only human and that they have their share of imperfections, but the question is how they handle their imperfections. And the reason that this can be so helpful is because these are tangible examples. In Paul's case, not only was he a tangible example of someone who was pursuing Christ with all of his heart, soul, mind, and strength, but he was also someone who cared deeply for the Philippians, and he was at least somewhat accessible to them. In what way was he instructing them to imitate him? In his journey of knowing and pursuing Jesus. It's not so much that they should learn to do everything the way that Paul does things; rather, it's that they should be united with Paul by having the common goal of pursuing Jesus

185

above everything else and demonstrating a commitment to growing in their love for Jesus and for one another.

The question that we must ask ourselves when we read this is whether or not we ourselves are worthy of having someone imitate us. If your children were to imitate you, can you honestly say that it would contribute to their growth in Christlikeness? If someone came in here right now and said, "I'm a Christian who is looking for someone to disciple me," would you feel worthy of volunteering?

We just went to see the movie "God's Not Dead" as a church, and in one of the scenes, the main character (Josh Wheaton) was trying to figure out if he should take up his philosophy professor's challenge to give evidence of God's existence. As he's struggling with this in a chapel, the pastor comes in and asks the Josh why he is troubled. After hearing about the challenge, the pastor says of Josh's classmates, "Your acceptance of this challenge may be the only meaningful exposure to God and Jesus they'll ever have." If your unsaved neighbors and co-workers do not see the Lord Jesus in you and the way that you live your life, they will, in all probability, never see Him and will never think twice about why they would need Him. Can people see your passion for Jesus in all that you do? If they were to imitate you, would they become more like Christ?

I'm not just trying to make anyone uncomfortable with this kind of question, but if you aren't comfortable with the idea of someone imitating your pursuit of Jesus, then you must also surely know what areas of your life you need to change in. So work on changing those areas . . . and bring someone alongside yourself to hold you accountable to those changes! There are no clauses in the Great Commission which state that you have to be perfect to be involved in the discipleship process. If there were, there would be no disciples!

Paul instructs the Philippians, "Keep your eyes on those who walk according to the example you have in us." He's talking about Timothy, Epaphroditus, and himself here, because they all were examples of people who had humbly reflected the nature of Christ by serving others self-sacrificially. Paul's instruction is to keep an eye on those who walk this way. Watch them, observe them, learn from them, and join them in humbly pursuing Jesus above all things. See how they press on in that pursuit, and press on with them. There's an implied intentionality here, because it's entirely possible to set our eyes on those who do NOT walk according to the example seen in the lives of Paul and other mature Christians. In fact, that is exactly what Paul is going to warn them of. First he told them whom they SHOULD keep their eyes on, and now he will tell them whom they should NOT keep their eyes on.

"For many, of whom I have often told you and now tell you even with tears, walk as enemies of the cross of Christ. Their end is destruction, their god is their belly, and they glory in their shame, with minds set on earthly things." (Philippians 3:18-19)

We are reminded here that we don't know the entire history between Paul and the Philippians, but he's making it clear here that at some point, he warned the Philippians of the many who walk as enemies of the cross. Perhaps he had written them another letter that didn't make its way into our Bibles. More likely than that is the possibility that he had warned them of this danger while he was among them.

One of the sub-themes of this chapter is that we must be on guard against both persons and ideas which are opposed to

187

the true Gospel which was given to the saints, once and for all. He's already warned us of them. Back in verse 2 of this third chapter, he warned us of these people he referred to as dogs, evildoers, and mutilators of the flesh. Between that point and this point, Paul has been discussing the importance of pursuing Jesus above all things, and how that process will be finalized when we're glorified in the presence of Christ one day. But now he turns his attention back to those who walk as enemies of the cross, so that he can show the distinction between our goal (which ends in our glorification) and the goal of those who walk as enemies of the Gospel, whose end is destruction.

As surely as there are those who are worthy of being imitated as they pursue Jesus, there are many more who must be shunned and rejected, because they walk as enemies of the cross. When the Gospel message is perverted in even the slightest bit, it is a threat to the well-being of the Church. We can sense that this is something that Paul is passionate about—so passionate, in fact, that he tells us that it brings him to tears to think about it, because the many of whom is he speaking are in danger of entering into eternity without saving faith.

There are two distinct types of enemies of the cross. First of all, there are those who seek to advance an atheistic, humanist philosophy. They don't believe in God—at least not on a conscious level. Romans 1 makes it clear that the only reason anyone falls into this position is because they have deliberately and intentionally suppressed the truth that they instinctively know about God. If you've ever met someone who passionately hates the very idea of there being a God (sometimes called an anti-theist), that type of person is an example of someone who walks as an enemy of the cross. This type of person is nowhere near as dangerous as the second type.

The second type of person who walks as an enemy of the cross is the pseudo-religious (those who follow a false religion). Maybe that means they're a Jehovah's Witness or a Scientologist, or maybe it means that they think they're a Christian, but the reality is that they're a false convert. These can be the most religiously-devout people you've ever met, but their lives are filled with bad fruit. They'll try to disguise their carnal desires for power and influence as being out-workings of their faith, and they love to put their good works out on display, but when you look at their lives, you see that it's not Christ that they're pursuing; rather it's desires of the flesh. Further, they're not looking to bring glory to Jesus through their good works; they're looking to bring glory to themselves. Jesus warned us of these people who might appear to be Christians but who are in reality false converts in Matthew 13 with the parable of the wheat and tares. These are the types of people that we must become aware of when we read the parable of the sower in Mark chapter 4—some seed gets devoured by birds, who represent the enemy of God, before they have a chance to take root. Some seed takes root, but the root is shallow, so the plant withers when the heat of the sun comes down upon it, representing those who fall away due to persecution or peer pressure. Some seed falls among thorns which destroy the plant before it can fully grow or take root, representing those who are drawn away from the Gospel by the deceitful desire for money or earthly treasure. And some seed falls on good soil, springing up and producing a harvest. The Judaizers that Paul warned us about back in verse 2 of the third chapter of Philippians would qualify as this type of enemy of the cross because of how they loved to put their works on display and pursued the desires of the flesh, disguising that pursuit as a pursuit for God. The fact that there are many who fall under this category explains why Paul told the Corinthians (2 Cor.

13:5) that they must examine their lives to see if they were truly in the faith—something that we must continually do as well. Paul describes those who fail this examination as such in his letter to Titus: "They profess to know God, but they deny him by their works. They are detestable, disobedient, unfit for any good work" (1:16). As surely as the one who either rejects or hates any idea of God is an enemy of the cross, this type of person is certainly an enemy of the cross as well.

What do these two types of people who walk as enemies of the Cross have in common? They're carnally-minded, and they embrace a set of corrupted, worldly values. The first principle from this passage is to look to mature Christians who are wholeheartedly pursuing Jesus, imitating them in their pursuit. In other words, look at the example of those who live first and foremost as citizens of Heaven. The second principle is that, as citizens of Heaven and earth, we must learn to shun worldly values, and that starts by not looking at those who embrace worldly values as people to be imitated.

Paul tells us four things about these people who are enemies of the Cross. First, he tells us that their end is destruction. This describes the majority of people, unfortunately. Jesus said, "Enter by the narrow gate. For the gate is wide and the way is easy that leads to destruction, and those who enter by it are many, for the gate is narrow and the way is hard that leads to life, and those who find it are few." (Matthew 7:13-14). Few are not headed for destruction, many are headed for destruction, because the road to destruction is easy, and the gate to destruction is pleasing to the flesh. These are people who are destined for an eternity in Hell, and they are not citizens of Heaven (even though they might tell you that they are). Some argue that Paul is making a case for what's called "annihilation," which is the belief that there is no literal hell. Rather, those who don't go to Heaven get destroyed, as in "removed from any type of existence whatsoever." However, the Greek word here is *apoleia*, really means "ruin," "waste," or "uselessness." The Greek word *aphanidzo* is the word that refers to the type of destruction that removes something from existence. That's the word that Jesus used when He said, "Do not lay up for yourselves treasures on earth, where moth and rust destroy" (Matthew 6:19). There's a significant difference. *Apoleia* and *aphanidzo* aren't even close to being the same word, and they don't refer to the same types of destruction. Those who are enemies of the cross are headed for eternal ruin.

Secondly, Paul tells us that their bellies are their gods. What does this mean? It means that they live a self-indulgent life, and they indulge themselves on whatever pleases their flesh: whether that be food or money or sex or what have you. It means that they worship the things that satisfy the physical desires of the flesh. When fulfilling hedonistic desires becomes the primary focus of a person's existence, it reveals that their proverbial "stomach" is their god.

Third, Paul tells us that they "glory in their shame." In other words, they boast of things that they shouldn't be very proud of. They're proud of things for which they should feel guilt and shame. Paul concludes the first chapter of Romans by listing off various types of wicked people, and he caps it all off by saying of those who have turned away from God, "Though they know God's righteous decree that those who practice such things deserve to die, they not only do them but give approval to those who practice them" (Romans 1:32). I think of people like Larry Flynt and Hugh Hefner—men who pioneered the pornography industry in this country, and they're proud of it! Rather than feeling shame as they should, they glory in what they have done. But Paul is talking about anyone who celebrates and glories in something that they should feel shame about. Maybe someone feels proud for stealing. Maybe they boast of how they've taken advantage of people. This is called "glorying in shame," and it describes those who are enemies of the Cross.

Fourth and finally, Paul tells us that those who are enemies of the cross have their minds set on earthly things. That's why Paul instructed the Colossian church, "Set your minds on things that are above, not on things that are on earth" (Col. 3:2). Do not set your mind on and imitate people whose treasure is here on earth, and who are not living first and foremost as citizens of heaven. Jesus said, "What does it profit a man to gain the whole world and forfeit his soul?" (Mark 8:36), but that doesn't seem to stop people from trying to have their best life now.

"But our citizenship is in heaven, and from it we await a Savior, the Lord Jesus Christ, who will transform our lowly body to be like his glorious body, by the power that enables him even to subject all things to himself." (Philippians 3:20-21)

Note the contrast that Paul starts with. He says, "But our citizenship." In other words, unlike those who live, walk, and operate as enemies who oppose the Gospel, we who are in Christ must recognize that our citizenship is, first and foremost, in heaven. Remember that the Philippians would have been proud to have been Roman citizens, but Paul is telling them that their Roman citizenship needed to be a given a distant second-place to their citizenship in heaven. In light of that truth, they needed to learn to see themselves as "aliens and strangers" who had their minds set on a greater country and kingdom than anything that this world has to offer. Paul is telling us that our citizenship in heaven isn't in the future; he's speaking in the present tense. He doesn't say "our citizenship WILL BE in heaven," he says "it IS in heaven." Our allegiance is first and foremost to the cross, not to a country—not to this country nor to any other country.

Friends, we are not of this world. We're in it, but we're not to be of it. We're just passing through. I once sat in the hospital room of a dying little girl who wanted to know why God would allow her to suffer and die, and all I could think to say is, "This world was never, ever, ever meant to be our permanent home. We weren't created for life on earth—we were created to experience eternal life in the presence of a God who loved us too much to allow us to find peace and fulfillment in this world, when He knows that only He can truly offer peace and fulfillment." We might not be facing a disease that will take our lives in the foreseeable future, but we nevertheless must all live with that type of perspective!

Those who were citizens of Rome were expected to live like Romans. We've all heard the saying, "When in Rome, do as the Romans do." That means living according to Roman values and interests. But Paul is saying, "When in Rome, don't just do what the unbelieving Romans are doing" just as surely as he would tell us, "When in America, don't just do what the unbelieving Americans are doing." Far too many Christians live in a way that demonstrates that they see themselves as citizens of the world who are loyal first and foremost to their country. They're still seeking earthly treasure and pleasure rather than living in light of their citizenship in heaven.

Paul reminds us that as citizens of heaven who are living like aliens and strangers in this world, there will be a day when Jesus will transform our lowly bodies to be like His glorious body. He's talking about the final step in the salvation process—glorification, which is the means by which we're separated from the presence of sin. Now, you might be wondering why I've been making such a big deal about the three stages of salvation. Why is it important that we recognize the differences between justification, sanctification, and glorification? First of all, if we don't recognize that justification and sanctification are different, we'll keep going back to the starting line (justification) rather than pressing forward, and that will hinder the way we're running the race (i.e., our sanctification). But a runner always runs the race with the goal in mind. Glorification is the goal of the Christian life. The day that we stand before Jesus, we will see Him as He really is, and we will become like Him in that the desires of the flesh will in no way appeal to us. As the apostle John tells us, "We know that when He appears we shall be like Him, because we shall see Him as He is" (1st John 3:2).

No matter what you're facing right now—no matter what mountains you might find yourself perched on, and no matter what valley you might be going through—it is all temporary. Whatever hardship, struggle, or temptation you might experience in your daily life, know that it will pass. So live for eternity as citizens of heaven, even in the here and now.

We saw back in chapter two that God exalted Jesus to the highest position as Lord of the Universe, with the name above all names, and that every knee will bow and every tongue will confess that Jesus is Lord. Just as Jesus humbled Himself and was exalted, He's coming again to exalt those who humbly pursue Him. We will be with Him, and we will become like Him. In light of that truth, we must resist the temptation to imitate those who live primarily as citizens of this world, seeking only to satisfy the desires of the flesh. Instead, imitate Paul and other mature Christians who are doing two things: 1) pursuing Jesus wholeheartedly, and 2) living as citizens of heaven on earth in eager anticipation of the return of Jesus, our glorious God and King, and the day in which He glorifies us, transforming us, as His people, into His very likeness.

~~~

Chapter 14: Peace in the Midst of Life's Warzones

Philippians 4:1-9

One of the first evangelical Christian churches I ever went to was held in downtown Los Angeles in a building that had been abandoned. Because it was in a rough area of town, it had been vandalized with spray paint. Gangs had once claimed this shell of a building as their territory, but the pastor had come in and cleaned it up a little bit so that his church could hold services there. And that was my first exposure to a Christian "slogan," if you will, with which we're probably all familiar. Across one of the side walls, in huge spray-painted letters, it read, "No Jesus, no peace. Know Jesus, know peace."

But what IS peace? In a nutshell, the world would define peace as the absence of conflict. How fitting that this slogan would be found in a church located in the trenches of conflict and war between rival gangs of Los Angeles in the early 90's.

But what is this peace that Jesus can bring us? In one sense, He brings us peace with Himself. Romans 5:1 says, "Therefore, since we have been justified by faith, we have peace with God through our Lord Jesus Christ." Peace with God is the purpose and the essence of the Gospel. Humanity had sinned, and every single one of us had fallen short of the glory of God. We had all violated the moral code that He wrote on the hearts of humanity. We had all committed what R.C. Sproul calls "cosmic treason," in that we had not only broken God's laws, but also in that we had tried to overthrow His reign over the universe every single time we sinned. And it was only by the atoning sacrifice of Jesus that God's wrath against our sin was fully satisfied. By His blood, those who have trusted in Jesus for their salvation are no longer at war with God. By faith in Jesus, we are justified and have peace with God. That's one sense of peace that we have through Jesus.

But what about peace in the warzones we call "daily life?" Countless false religions have been founded in the pursuit of peace in our daily lives, and they—along with multiple pop-psychology sources—would have us believe that we have to get rid of the things in our lives which cause anxiety. If peace is the absence of conflict and problems, and if conflict and problems are an inescapable part of life (as I truly believe it is), how are we to find some sense of peace for our daily lives? Do we eliminate the sources of conflict, stress, and anxiety altogether? Does one need to divorce their spouse and throw the kids out? Does one need to quit their job to get away from a boss who has the personality of a hungry snake? It was the famous English novelist and writer Virginia Woolf who once wrote, "You cannot find peace by avoiding life." There is so much truth in that statement. The reality is that we can't find peace by simply getting rid of the things that cause us problems and anxiety. Peace isn't found by cleaning our lives of problems and troubles—those things are inescapable. Peace isn't found by avoiding the storms and valleys of life. The best we can do is **wish** that we could exert that much control over our lives. What we're going to see today is that true peace can be found in the midst of the storms, and in the middle of the warzones of life, and that it comes by setting our minds on the things that God wants us to set our minds on.

As we turn in our bibles to the final chapter of the book of Philippians, we see that the first thing that Paul writes is this:

"Therefore, my brothers, whom I love and long for, my joy and crown, stand firm thus in the Lord, my beloved." (Philippians 4:1)

The word "therefore" is always significant. What it tells us is to do something in light of what has been written in the context immediately prior to the word. So when Paul says "therefore," he means "because we're pursuing Jesus with all of our hearts, souls, minds, and strength, counting Him more worthy than anything and everything that this world has to offer, and because we're living as citizens of heaven in the here and now," our lives should be different in some way. If I'm being honest, I think that it may be a mistake for the people who divided our Bibles into chapters and verses to have put this verse in the next chapter, because it's so closely connected to everything that we studied in the previous chapter. At the same time, however, this one verse leads us into a new way of living, which is one of the things that we're going to be talking about in this chapter.

So because we're pursuing Jesus, pressing on despite our failures and shortcomings, and because we recognize that our citizenship is first and foremost of heaven, Paul tells us that we must stand firm in the Lord.

It's interesting that Paul uses this metaphor of standing firm, given that in the previous chapter, he used the metaphor of running. It's like life is an obstacle course, and our job is to press on in the race in our pursuit of Jesus, even when we stumble. So which is it: are we running or are we standing? Are we to press forward full steam ahead, or are we to stay right where we are? The answer is both. We press on through the obstacles in life—the failures, the moments of weakness, the inadequacies, the challenges to our faith—but the secret to doing that successfully is in standing strong—firm—in what we believe and strive toward. The goal doesn't change because the promises of God don't change. The promises of God don't change because God Himself doesn't change. Jesus has redeemed a people for Himself—a people whose standing before God isn't based on their works, but on the work of Jesus on Calvary. The peace that we have between ourselves and God is established, promised, and unchanging. This is the foundation of the Christian life. Stand on it, because it will not and it cannot be moved.

Jesus said, "Everyone then who hears these words of mine and does them will be like a wise man who built his house on the rock. And the rain fell, and the floods came, and the winds blew and beat on that house, but it did not fall, because it had been founded on the rock. And everyone who hears these words of mine and does not do them will be like a foolish man who built his house on the sand. And the rain fell, and the floods came, and the winds blew and beat against that house, and it fell, and great was the fall of it" (Matthew 7:24-27). There will be temptations to build parts of our lives on the solid, unshakable foundation of Jesus, but to build parts of our lives on a different foundation—one that will give way. We must resist that temptation, because if you have a house with two different foundations, one that moves, and one that doesn't move, the whole house will be ripped in half. That's the very antithesis of finding peace in life!

The secret of the Christian life is to build everything we have on Jesus, standing firm in the sense that we're never swaying, never daring to set foot on the sinking sands which appeal so strongly to us. When we do this, we will have the strength to run the race well. So these two metaphors are not so contrary or paradoxical after all.

But the peace that we have with God must filter through to other aspects of our lives. Being in right relationship with God should cause us to strive to live in right relationship with God's people. Knowing that two of the women leaders in the Philippian church were at odds with one another, Paul therefore continues by writing:

"I entreat Euodia and I entreat Syntyche to agree in the Lord." (Philippians 4:2)

I have to be honest—this translation from the ESV is somewhat lacking. "Agree in the Lord"—what exactly does that mean? Agree on what's for breakfast? Agree that Jesus is Lord (they already agreed on that)? My opinion is that the same Greek word should typically be translated to the same English word, unless the context changes. This is the same word that Paul used back in 2:2 when he instructed the Philippians, "complete my joy by being of the same mind." In fact, it's the same two-word combination. Why do the ESV translators render one to say "same mind" and the other to say "agree?" Who knows . . . but their translation of this verse is far too ambiguous. Paul is specifically calling these two women out, instructing them to apply to themselves the principle from 2:2 to be "of the same mind."

These two ladies hadn't divided the church yet, but we all know that when feuding begins, it doesn't take long for people to take sides, and so the moment conflict arises, division is on the horizon. This isn't new for us—we've already covered this principle. All I wish to do at this point is re-emphasize the fact that unity among Christian brethren is not optional—it's mandatory. The love that we demonstrate for our fellow brothers and sisters in Christ is one of the primary evidences of a person's true conversion. That makes this a black and white issue. The apostle John put it in that type of language for us, telling us, "Whoever says he is in the light and hates his brother is still in darkness. Whoever loves his brother abides in the light, and in him there is no cause for stumbling." (1 Jn. 2:9-10). We can't help but notice that there is no room to wiggle in that statement; there is no greyness to cloud our understanding. If you demonstrate love toward your Christian brethren, you will have provided strong evidence of your position in Christ. On the contrary, if you fail—or, for whatever reason, you outright *refuse*—to demonstrate love toward your Christian brethren, you've provided strong evidence that you are **not** positioned in Christ. As Paul Washer writes, "The one who demonstrates a real and enduring love for his brother in Christ and for the church collectively gives powerful evidence of conversion. However, the one who claims Christ and yet does not love his brother has little grounds for such a boast" (Washer, "Gospel Assurance & Warnings," p. 59).

Please don't blow this off and dismiss the warning here without taking a moment to consider your own affections toward other Christians. This is a very serious warning for anyone who claims Christ, because when a person is born again, God will change their affections to match His affections. James said this: "What causes quarrels and what causes fights among you? Is it not this, that your passions are at war within you?" (James 4:1). One of the first changes God makes in a person is He gives them a love for their fellow brethren. That's why Jesus said, "A new commandment I give to you, that you love one another: just as I have loved you, you also are to love one another. By this all people will know that you are my

201

disciples, if you have love for one another" (John 13:34-35). God loves His people, and thus, if you don't love His people, your affections haven't been changed. If your affections haven't been changed, you should be smitten with fear to the point that you can't help but fall to your knees and beg God to change your affections and to place a love for God's people in your heart.

Please understand this much: if you want to know how to both love your fellow brethren AND find peace in the warzones of life, you must understand that exercising forgiveness toward others is crucial to both loving others and living in peace. Jesus told us how important forgiveness toward each other was in the parable of the unforgiving slave (Matthew 18:21-35), which ends with a very serious warning for us to consider: that God the Father will not forgive those who refuse to forgive others. That's because bitterness is so destructive for the person who holds it. Paul tells us that love "does not take into account a wrong *suffered*" (1st Corinthians 13:5). That means letting go of the offense and forgiving without conditions.

The serious nature of this issue explains why Paul is calling these two specific individuals out. We don't know what the situation was, but we know that whatever was done could not be undone. Paul didn't dare presume that he could undo whatever had happened. But he could encourage them to change their attitudes toward one another in regards to the situation. They needed to stop waiting for the other to make the first apology or concession. He's calling them to follow Christ's example by deciding to be willfully humble and self-sacrificial. We've known from the beginning that this is the point that Paul was working toward. But what he says next is very important for all of us.

"Yes, I ask you also, true companion, help these women, who have labored side by side with me in the gospel together with Clement and the rest of my fellow workers, whose names are in the book of life." (Philippians 4:3)

Isn't it sad that these two had labored side by side with Paul and his team of missionaries, and that it had all led to this? There were people who were heaven-bound because of the work that these two women had done together. How huge is that? It's enormous! But they had lost their perspective. They had stopped living like citizens of heaven, as they got side-tracked by this disagreement. And I think that we can be fairly confident that they weren't fighting over something that was eternally significant. If that had been the case, I'm confident that Paul would have stepped in and taken one side or another. Do you know how rare it is for Christians to divide over something that actually is of eternal significance? We divide over things like preferences and personality differences much more frequently than we divide over something that actually matters. That doesn't mean you shouldn't voice your opinion, but it does mean that if and when things don't go your way (as they sometimes won't), don't allow bitterness to fester, because when that happens, you'll not only destroy the relationship with the other person, but you'll destroy your own witness. Another thing that 1st Corinthians 13:5 tells us is that love does not insist on getting its own way. We exist to bring glory to Jesus— period. That's the priority; don't fall for the temptation to lose sight of it. Unforgiveness and bitterness will prevent you from aiming at the right goal, and they're incompatible with the love we are to demonstrate to our fellow brothers and sisters in Christ.

But there's something else in this verse that I think is very significant. Paul encourages someone he refers to as "true companion" to help these two women to resolve the conflict. There are a couple of possible options we have when we try to discover the identity of this person. The first option is that Paul was addressing someone whose name literally meant "true companion" or "fellow worker." In that case, the person's name was Syzygus. Or maybe Paul was referring to Epaphroditus, who was the deliverer of the letter to the church in Philippi. Or maybe Paul meant to address this to everyone in the church who had a chance to read this letter or hear it read. Whatever the case, most people try to stay out of the middle of conflicts like this one, but conflict happens, so it's sometimes necessary for someone to step in as a mediator. Just like Christ gives us peace with God, the person who mediates gives peace to the body of Christ.

Paul adds that those who worked with him have their names written in the book of life. That's a great reminder that we'd better resolve our differences and resolve to work together in peace, because we're all going to be with one another in eternity!

What causes fights and quarrels among the brethren? Conflicting desires within us. Conflict with others really stems from conflict within ourselves. So where are we to turn to resolve these conflicts within ourselves? Paul is going to address that now, as he continues by writing,

"Rejoice in the Lord always; again I will say, rejoice! Let your gentle spirit be known to all men. The Lord is near. Be anxious for nothing, but in everything by prayer and supplication with thanksgiving let your requests be made known to God. And the peace of God, which surpasses all comprehension, will guard your hearts and your minds in Christ Jesus." (Philippians 4:4-7, NASB)

It's very odd that a man who has been beaten and imprisoned is encouraging us to rejoice as strongly as Paul is. But that fact reveals a very important principle for us: that peace isn't something to be found only in ideal circumstances. Peace isn't something that is only found in the absence of conflict or storms or valleys or trials. Rather, true peace is found in looking to and pursuing Jesus. Our outward circumstances don't have to affect our inward attitudes. Peace is found in keeping an eternal perspective on things, which starts with knowing that Jesus gave His life for you, He took God's wrath for you, and He is with you always! So rejoice in the Lord, always. Always! It's almost as if Paul anticipates the response: "Oh, but Paul . . . you don't understand how hard my circumstances are!" Really? Are we really going to go there?

It's easy to get discouraged about conflict or unpleasant circumstances. With the consumerist mindset of Western culture, it's so easy to get mad when we don't get things done our way. But for the Christian, the cross is always the cure for conflict, and the cross is always the cure for discouragement. Paul was anything BUT a hypocrite in giving this instruction.

Similarly, he instructs them to let their "gentle spirit" be apparent. The Greek word here can also be translated as "gentleness." The word is really expressing the essence of a spirit that is fair-minded and charitable, ready and willing to surrender their own rights and privileges as a means of demonstrating a deep, caring, gentle consideration for others, even (or maybe especially) when we may feel that others don't necessarily deserve to be treated with gentleness. What a wonderful quality to have in the midst of conflict or trials! You see, joy isn't always evident to people, because true joy is an internal experience.

Gentleness, on the other hand, is the fruit of joy. It's like a clock: all you see is the face, but behind the face are all of these gears that are working together. That's how our collective gentleness is to be seen as well—it starts with sharing a common joy, which causes us to work together, producing something that is observable about our works.

Now, let's just be honest about how relationships work. It will be easy to be gentle with some people, and it will feel absolutely impossible with others. Paul says that we must demonstrate gentleness toward everyone—whether that's our Christian brethren or unbelievers. And the Holy Spirit is the only source of strength that's powerful enough to ensure that you're capable of demonstrating gentleness with those with whom gentleness doesn't come easily.

Gentleness is the fruit of a life that is fully surrendered to Jesus. If you have kept part of your life compartmentalized—that is, if you have decided that there's a part of your life that Jesus doesn't have Lordship over—you cannot experience the type or degree of peace that you could if you would just give it all to Him. That means your job, it means your relationships, it means your fears, your failures, your struggles, your victories— yielding every aspect of your life to Jesus. That's why Paul instructs us to let our requests be made known to God through prayer and supplication with thanksgiving. God is strong enough to answer whatever your prayer is, and He's active in our lives, causing all things to work together as a means of growing us in Christlikeness. So when our prayers are answered as we had hoped, praise the Lord! And when our prayers aren't answered as we had hoped, praise the Lord then as well! Put it all in His hands, and trust Him with it. When we do that, Paul says, the peace of God, which surpasses all understanding, will be a reality in our lives. The question is whether or not we'll trust God and yield every aspect of our lives to Him, and whether or not we'll do that consistently.

When a person is willing to consistently yield every aspect of their life to God, that person can be used in mighty ways by God, because they don't fear rejection or punishment or shame of any kind. That person doesn't get tripped up by pride, because they walk humbly before the Lord. That person throws all of their anxiety and despair on Him, simply trusting that God is both good and powerful. Here's a painful dose of reality that we've probably all had to choke down at one time or another: God can change your circumstances when you're in some type of a conflict or going through a trial, but He's more interested in changing you!

I've learned to thank God for the trials I've been through, just as I've learned to thank Him for conflict, because it's all taught me to rely on Jesus. It's taught me that His ways are better than my ways. It's taught me that my sense of peace is contingent on my standing with Jesus, and nothing else! And so when I look back on hardships and trials, I don't count myself as a victim, as so many go through life doing; rather, I count myself a recipient of a deep and profound blessing, because God accepts me and has used (and continues to use) those things to make me more like Jesus. And therefore I am thankful for those hardships! And as I become thankful for what God has done in the past, I don't find anything in the present or future to be anxious about, because I've had a front row seat to seeing Him get me through impossible situations before. You can go through life seeing yourself as a victim, or you can go through life seeing yourself as a victor in Christ Jesus. When you chose the latter option, you will have a peace about yourself that those who are not in Christ Jesus find unthinkable and unfathomable. But it's yours, if you'll simply trust that God is good, sovereign, and all-powerful, and remember that because you've placed your faith in Jesus, God is now causing all things to work together to mold you, and to shape you, and to conform you to the likeness of Jesus.

You see, we don't find peace when the conflicts or problems of life are gone. Rather, we find peace when we understand that God has given us everything we could possibly need to handle the difficult circumstances we face in daily life. That's why we have access to a peace that the world has no logical, psychological, or sociological explanation for! Paul knew that this was one of those things that you can read books about, you can attend motivational conferences about, and you can watch in the lives of others, and still not be able to fully understand it without experiencing it first-hand. It is above and beyond human comprehension or understanding. And this peace will guard our hearts and minds in Christ Jesus. It's like an impenetrable fortress that protects us from whatever life might throw in our direction.

Now, you might read this, and think to yourself, "I've tried all of these things, but to no avail. Why can't I find or experience this peace that Paul is talking about?" The answer very well may be the types of things you allow into your mind. Paul continues, writing,

"Finally, brothers, whatever is true, whatever is honorable, whatever is just, whatever is pure, whatever is lovely, whatever is commendable, if there is any excellence, if there is anything worthy of praise, think about these things. What you have learned and received and heard and seen in me—practice these things, and the God of peace will be with you." (Philippians 4:8-9)

I usually can't stand using alliteration—using a series of words which begin with the same letter, such as "always avoid alliteration,"—but pessimism prohibits peace. How often do you find yourself thinking that you WOULD do things God's way, but you're afraid of how it might turn out? Or you would do what you feel like the Holy Spirit is prompting you to do, but you back away because you know that it won't be easy? Now, I don't believe in the power of positive thinking in the way that pop-psychology promotes it, but there is a place for positive thinking in the life of the Christian.

I love that Paul starts with "whatever is true." In other words, accept things the way they are. Don't pretend that things are different than they really are, and quit wishing that things were different than they are. That's just a waste of brain capacity, and when it comes to conflict, all that does is put a proverbial elephant in the room—something that makes everything feel tense and awkward and uncomfortable. Reality is the foundation for positive thinking, and it prevents positive thinking from turning into wishful thinking.

From there, look for things that are honorable, just, pure, lovely, commendable, excellent, worthy of praise, and set your mind on these types of things. Sinful actions stem from sinful thoughts, and sinful thoughts will prevent us from experiencing the peace that passes understanding. The only way to overcome the thoughts that steal your peace is to replace them with something positive. Notice that Paul doesn't simply instruct us to set our minds on what makes us happy—because sometimes the wrong things can give us a sense of happiness. Rather, set your mind on what makes you holy, and you'll learn to find happiness in that holiness.

The truth is that the battle for peace is won or lost in our minds. Back in verse 3, Paul instructed these two people who were wrapped up in conflict to be like-minded. Then he showed us how the right attitude toward each other and our circumstances can bring us a depth of peace that the world knows nothing about. And here he's saying that we must put a filter on what we allow into our thoughts. And look what Paul ends this passage with. He says that we must put these things into practice. We must actively and intentionally do them. Our actions reveal our trust in God, and our actions reveal to everyone around us that the power of God is with us as His people to resolve every conflict and to deliver us into peace in the warzones of life.

~~~

Chapter 15: Christis Beyond Sufficient

Philippians 4:10-23

With this chapter, we will conclude our study of the marvelous epistle that was written by Paul to the Philippians while he was chained to a Roman guard. There is no other book in all of the Bible which so clearly outlines the manner in which we are to regard one another. As we started this study, I told you that the theme of the book was two-fold—that it's about growing in our love for Jesus and for one another. This two-fold theme has been fleshed out and unfolded in order that we can very easily apply these principles to our own lives today, almost 2,000 years after it was written. Throughout this somewhat short epistle (at least short in comparison to his letters to the Romans and the Corinthians), Paul has used the word "rejoice" a total of eleven times. That's because the key to growing in our love for Jesus and for each other is to rejoice in the Lord—always!

The question is: what will keep us rejoicing, no matter what may come, and regardless of what our circumstances may be? The answer is found in understanding the all-sufficiency of Christ. He died in our place in order that we may be forgiven by God's grace, justified through faith in Him. But justification, as we've seen, is merely the starting line. Christ was more than sufficient for our justification, but He's more than sufficient for our sanctification as well. He is more than sufficient to overcome whatever may come. He is more than sufficient to get us through the storms and valleys of life. He is more than sufficient to strengthen us when we face circumstances that are beyond our ability to control. The more we trust in His sufficiency, the more we rejoice as we look to Him—always! And what we find when we do that is that our attitudes change, our perspective of difficult circumstances changes, and our perspective about conflict is turned upside-down.

Paul starts out our passage at hand by telling us what happened to him when he looked beyond his circumstances and learned to apply these principles to his own life.

"I rejoiced in the Lord greatly that now at length you have revived your concern for me. You were indeed concerned for me, but you had no opportunity. Not that I am speaking of being in need, for I have learned in whatever situation I am to be content. I know how to be brought low, and I know how to abound. In any and every circumstance, I have learned the secret of facing plenty and hunger, abundance and need." (Philippians 4:10-11)

While Paul never stayed tied down in one place for too long, he had a team of people who came from place to place with him, as Paul planted multiple churches deep into Gentile territory. While we know that he worked as a tent-maker to help support himself, it wasn't enough to sustain Paul and all of his ministry team. In his first letter to the Thessalonians, he was emphatic that he didn't come in and burden them with his needs, writing, "For you remember, brothers, our labor and toil: we worked night and day, that we might not be a burden to any of you, while we proclaimed to you the gospel of God" (1st Thess. 2:9). He wanted to make clear to them that he wasn't preaching the gospel for financial gain.

Paul made a similar point to the Corinthians. In
1 st Corinthians 9:11-18, Paul made it clear that he
deliberately refused any gifts from the Corinthians because
he didn't want them to think that he was seeking financial
gain. In the midst of that passage, however, he does make
it clear that the church body has a God-ordained
responsibility to support and meet the needs of those who
were ministering to them.

People get really uneasy when it comes to talking about
money in church, but the reality is that ministry takes time
and resources, and without money, most ministry wouldn't
be able to happen. Here we see that Paul knew this
principle to be true as well. The Philippians had been
concerned for the sustenance of Paul's ministry, but until
now, didn't have a way to express their support in a
tangible way. We're not sure what had prevented them
from supporting him prior to this point. It may have been
as simple as location—the Philippians were a long ways
away from Rome, and there were no federally-funded mail
services. But when the opportunity presented itself, they
acted on it. So Paul rejoiced upon learning of their
renewed support and concern for the sustenance of his
ministry.

But look at what Paul follows that up with. He writes, "Not
that I am speaking of being in need, for I have learned in
whatever situation I am to be content." He hadn't
expressed his need. He didn't solicit money from them (or
from anyone). Why not? Because he knew that he would
find a way to be content with his situation, whether that
meant living on the streets or sleeping in the finest 5-star
hotels in the world. That's because the secret to being
content isn't found in our circumstances.

If you watch the news much, it seems like there's always some poll or another in which someone is trying to measure how content people are. In fact, there's something called the "Happiness Index." We've heard of the Gross National Product, but have you heard of the Gross National Happiness? That's a real thing! Gallup ranks states by how happy each respective state's citizens are. One of the most interesting things about the Happiness Index is that if you look at it historically, the ups and downs follow the economic state of the nation. How interesting! People's happiness is connected closely to money. But Paul's wasn't. Paul is telling us that he has learned the secret to contentedness, regardless of his circumstances.

Notice that he said that he has *learned* to be content. You see, this is not one of those things that comes naturally to us. We are born into a system which raises us to believe that more is better, and that we must always strive for more. Like us, Paul was surely born with a sense of discontentment. But did that change overnight when he converted to Christianity? No, he had to learn it. How? By experiencing hardship and success alike, and learning to look beyond his circumstances to the Lord Jesus, who is beyond sufficient. If He is truly Lord of all, then He has the power to provide for us. If He's really all-powerful, He could change our circumstances. But He's not just a cosmic sugar daddy who gives us whatever we want. He's more interested in our holiness than He is in our happiness, and He demonstrates more power by changing **us** than He would by simply changing our circumstances. That's the miracle of transformation.

The point is that if we trust that the Lord is sovereign over our lives, then we trust that He has the power to change our circumstances. So when our circumstances don't change, how can we complain or feel discontent if we truly believe that God is causing all things to work together for our good—which is, ultimately, our growth in Christ's likeness (Romans 8:28-29)? If we truly believe that nothing can come against us because God is for us, then we won't ever have a reason to feel discontent about anything!

Remember back in the second chapter when Paul told the Philippian Christians to do all things without grumbling or complaining? What we learned there is that this is an issue of attitude and trust. Contentment, conversely, is really found in our attitude and our trust in God. And so if we want to feel content with life, no matter what our circumstances might be, we must either learn to see things from God's perspective (which is a legitimate possibility sometimes) and just trust in God's goodness and His sovereignty. If you want to experience contentment the way Paul did, remember that nothing is yours—it's all God's—and so what we have temporary possession of is a gift. So trust in God to meet your needs, and be a good and faithful steward with what He's entrusted you with. True contentment is not getting everything you could possibly want; it's feeling satisfied and thankful with whatever you have. That's the lesson that Paul learned over time.

Look at what the psalmist wrote in one of the most beautiful descriptions of God's providence in all of Scripture:

"You visit the earth and water it; You greatly enrich it;
the river of God is full of water; You provide their grain,
for so You have prepared it.
You water its furrows abundantly, settling its ridges,
softening it with showers, and blessing its growth.
You crown the year with your bounty;
your wagon tracks overflow with abundance." (Psalm 65:9-

11)

And Jesus, knowing how God provides for even the sparrows, which were sold two for a penny, proclaimed, "Fear not, therefore; you are of more value than many sparrows" (Matthew 10:31). This was a principle that Paul applied to his life. He trusted God's goodness, he trusted God's sovereign providence, and in that, he found contentment, even in the midst of desperate circumstances. One of the hardest lessons we must learn is that we're not in control of our lives. But God is. That's a lesson that we have to learn over and over and over again. But it's also one of the most valuable lessons we can learn, and I don't know if there's any lesson we can learn that can bring more peace than that one. That's why Paul is thankful instead of bitter!

Understand this context, because it's what leads us up to one of the most misused verses in all of Scripture. You have undoubtedly heard it and seen it, if you watch sports.

"I can do all things through Him who strengthens me."
(Philippians 4:13)

A few years ago, Tim Tebow was constantly in the limelight of the football field, and when the camera would zoom in on him, the audience could see that this verse was written in the black paint under his. Jon Jones, the light-heavyweight champion of the UFC, has the verse tattooed on his chest. Like Tebow and Jones, countless Christian athletes recite this verse as if they're summoning power from a mystical power reserve that can be tapped into when the odds are against them or when an enemy needs to be defeated. In that sense, it's not all that different from the cartoon character He-Man, who would pull out his sword and say, "By the power of Greyskull, I have the power!"

Or maybe we could liken it to Iron Man—Tony Stark is just an average guy, but when you put the Iron Man gear on him, he's practically invincible!

Countless proponents of the false gospel of prosperity use this verse to support the idea that God will give you whatever you want, whenever you want, just by believing this verse. I have to wonder—how do they explain starving children in third world countries? I mean, couldn't these false teachers just believe this verse and solve the problem?

This is "believe it and receive it" or "name it and claim it" theology. Implicit in this type of thinking is that if you want a raise at work, just believe this verse, and it will happen. *Cha-ching!* Do you want to make that big sale? No problem. Believe that you can do all things through Christ, and it will happen. *Cha-ching!* You want to be healed of a sickness or disease? You can do it through Christ who strengthens you. Yeah, right—we all know that that's not how it works. Friends, this type of understanding of this verse is nonsense! Was Paul saying that he can do all things through Christ because he was boldly embracing all of the riches and rewards and material blessings that God was heaping upon him? Was Paul talking about reaching new heights and doing impossible things? Or was he saying it because he knew that by looking to and pursuing Jesus, he could overcome the crushing and devastating feelings of despair when he *didn't* reach the new heights he had hoped to, and he wasn't receiving the blessings that he had wanted and maybe even prayed for?

Paul wrote this as he was chained to a Roman guard while he was starving to death because nobody was supporting him while he was imprisoned. Unlike the American prison system, the Romans didn't necessarily provide meals for prisoners—they often had to pay for it themselves. He certainly was not having one material blessing after another piled on top of him. And so Paul wasn't encouraging the Philippians to go out and crush the adversary; rather, he was encouraging them to press on and trust in the Lord even when it feels like the adversary is crushing them!

As one commentator notes, this verse is "not really about who has the strength to play to the best of their abilities in a sporting contest…. This verse is about having strength to be content when we are facing those moments in life when physical resources are minimal" (Bargerhuff, E., *The Most Misused Verses in the Bible*). This verse is about the abundant sufficiency of Christ working in and through us, and how we can be content and avoid feeling discouraged when it feels like the world is just beating us down.

When pastor Matt Chandler came down with brain cancer a few years back, he said something that shocked me. He said that he counted it as a blessing and honor that God would allow him to go through the fight against cancer in order that the glory and power of God could be on display in his life. He knew that there was a possibility that the cancer might win (praise the Lord, it didn't), but he wasn't going to let it stop him from trusting in God's goodness. That's the type of attitude—the type of mentality—that Paul is talking about! You see, sometimes God allows us to go through trials in order that His all-sustaining power can be demonstrated through us! And so, in that sense, to find ourselves in difficult circumstances is actually to be blessed abundantly!

Don't ever forget what Paul wrote to the Corinthians: "You are not your own, for you were bought with a price. So glorify God in your body" (1st. Cor. 6:19-20). That means that God is the one who is in charge of our lives, and accepting that fact with no conditions will free us to have the right attitude about our circumstances, whether we're rich or poor, healthy or ill, young or old. We may have much or we may have little; either way, the issue is whether or not we are acting on the belief that this is what God has ordained for this season of our lives.

Paul now answers a question that most of us have probably asked before, or which you've maybe been wondering about as we've been leading up to this point: "how does God provide for our every need?"

"Yet it was kind of you to share my trouble. And you Philippians yourselves know that in the beginning of the gospel, when I left Macedonia, no church entered into partnership with me in giving and receiving, except you only. Even in Thessalonica you sent me help for my needs once and again." (Philippians 4:14-16)

First, we see that the Philippians shared in his troubles. There is a very, very important principle behind this, and every single one of us needs to understand this: *God often blesses His people through His people.* Could God have made a few hundred bucks suddenly show up in Paul's hands? Sure He could have. But why would He do that, when the same thing can end up in Paul's hands by God laying the conviction on the hearts of others and allowing them to act on that conviction? Not to mention the fact that it teaches them to be sensitive to the leading of the Holy Spirit in their lives. It seems clear to me that it kills two or three birds with one stone, so to speak, for God to choose the latter. God loves to use His people to accomplish His purposes, no matter how small or insignificant they might feel in the big picture!

So what we see is that there was something of a partnership with the Philippians that no other church wanted to have with him, which started almost immediately after Paul arrived in Philippi to plant the church. Paul planted their church community, he taught them, and ministered to them and served as a blessing from God to them, and in return, they blessed Paul with financial support. He provided for them and blessed them spiritually, and they provided for him and blessed him materially.

I am always very hesitant to describe my ministry as "my ministry." It's not just mine. It's first and foremost the Lord's, of course. I play a small part in it, but without support, it couldn't happen. And so anything that I do, I consider to be shared. For example, when it comes to those who support my podcasting ministry, I count it as their ministry too.

While people get uncomfortable when you talk about ministry and money, Jesus had a ton to say about money. In fact, maybe the reason that people get so uncomfortable when ministry and money come up is because money is God's top competition for our hearts. The truth very well may be that it's only the people who love and worship money that get so uptight about discussing ministry and money. And maybe what makes those people feel uncomfortable is the fact that they can feel the Lord trying to pry it out of their hands. But the New Testament principle of giving is summed up in what Paul wrote in his second letter to the Corinthians: "Each one must give as he has decided in his heart, not reluctantly or under compulsion, for God loves a cheerful giver" (9:7).

That brings us to a second principle that's implied here: *it's a blessing to bless others.* The Philippians were not only blessing Paul; they blessed the entire church in

220

Thessalonica, because they supported Paul while he was ministering there. They were not only blessing Paul, they were also blessing anyone who was touched by Paul's ministry. Guess what? That means that the Philippians blessed us. If they hadn't supported Paul's ministry, he wouldn't have had occasion to write them this letter, which has blessed innumerable people over the centuries! When we have the right attitude about giving, we find that it is a blessing to bless others.

Paul closes with a beautiful benediction, writing:

"Not that I seek the gift, but I seek the fruit that increases to your credit. I have received full payment, and more. I am well supplied, having received from Epaphroditus the gifts you sent, a fragrant offering, a sacrifice acceptable and pleasing to God. And my God will supply every need of yours according to His riches in glory in Christ Jesus. To our God and Father be glory forever and ever. Amen." (Philippians 4:17-20)

I love that Paul says, "Not that I seek the gift." This is his way of telling the Philippians that it wasn't all about him and what he needed. He says instead that "I seek the fruit that increases to **your** credit." What he means is that they are investing in God's kingdom, and they are storing up treasure in heaven, where moth and rust do not destroy. The fruit is like a dividend that they will reap in their heavenly account. I've heard preachers say, "We give to get to give to get." That's purely selfish. We do not give in order that God will give back to us. Rather, we give because God has already given to us, and we understand that God often blesses His people through His people and that for the Christian who understands how greatly God has blessed them, it's a blessing to bless others.

Was God going to reward the Philippians with earthly treasure? Maybe . . . or maybe not. That's God's call. He can sovereignly decide how He will bless and reward them. But our flesh so badly wants God to bless us materially! And sometimes He will, and sometimes He won't. When He doesn't, maybe it's to teach us to learn what a blessing it is to bless others, rather than doing it for selfish gain! Notice that Paul does NOT say that "God will supply every need of yours according to His riches in money." He does NOT say that "God will supply every need of yours according to His riches in material possessions or positions of power and influence." No, he says that "God will supply every need of yours according to His riches in GLORY" (emphasis added).

It's important for us to realize that while Philippi was a fairly well-to-do city, many of those in the church had lost much of the affluence they had once had when they converted to Christianity. Paul wrote something else to the Corinthians that we should take note of:

"We want you to know, brothers, about the grace of God that has been given among the churches of Macedonia, for in a severe test of affliction, their abundance of joy and their extreme poverty have overflowed in a wealth of generosity on their part. For they gave according to their means, as I can testify, and beyond their means, of their own accord, begging us earnestly for the favor of taking part in the service of the saints." (2nd Corinthians 8:1-4)

A lot of people say, "Oh, I'll give more when I've got more." Really? That's not how it works, and we all know it, because it's not about what's in our bank accounts; it's about what's in our hearts. And so as Paul closes out his letter to the Philippians by saying that God will supply every need of theirs, he doesn't mean that God is going to just drop a pile of cash in their laps. Maybe He will, or maybe He won't. But they can be content because they are in Christ, who has blessed His people with every heavenly blessing even in the present, and He alone is sufficient to meet our every need. Maybe that means giving them the courage to face a desperate state of poverty . . . or death. Christ is a reward that is greater than any earthly treasure! God's job is not to be the cosmic genie who gives us everything we want, but He has promised to give us everything that we need to live for Him and to reflect His glory in our actions and our attitudes.

Finally, Paul adds something of a post-script after this benediction. The purpose of this letter had been to bring the community of Christians back together, and thus he adds the finishing touches by writing:

"Greet every saint in Christ Jesus. The brothers who are with me greet you. All the saints greet you, especially those of Caesar's household. The grace of the Lord Jesus Christ be with your spirit." (Philippians 4:21-23)

The Christians in Rome, and specifically and (especially) those who were in Caesar's household sent their greetings along with this letter, implying that they were all linked together by a common identity in Christ. They were very different people—the church has always consisted of very different types of people from all demographics and social strata. Here's something that's interesting: in Roman culture, one could be put to death for expressing a loyalty to Christ over Caesar. Yet, some of those in Caesar's very household were among the saints. They had given their loyalty to Jesus instead of Caesar. How could they send their greetings without being discovered and facing the consequences of having a higher loyalty to Christ than to Caesar? There's only one way that makes perfect sense:

the guard that was watching over Paul was very likely among them! This awful situation that Paul was in had a greater purpose. That guard needed to hear the gospel, and the only way for that to happen was to chain Paul to him. Remember that, the next time you're going through a trial. Remember that there may be a higher purpose to your circumstances that you won't see until you can look back on it.

Paul had been in an awful situation, but he had made the most of it, and he was storing up treasure in heaven because of it. Paul has shared the secret of finding peace and joy even in the ugliest circumstances: it's found in our pursuit and imitation of Christ, and in our commitment to serving one another as fellow Christians. If the Philippians could only do the same things, applying the principles that Paul has expressed and taught throughout this letter, they too could feel content, no matter what situation or circumstances they faced, as they grew in their love for Jesus and for one another.

~~~

About the Author

Toby Logsdon is the Senior Pastor of New Beginnings Church in Lynnwood, Washington, and is the founder and director of BibleStudyPodcasts.Org. After spending many years in the casino industry of Las Vegas, Toby felt the call to ministry and moved across the country to Charlotte, NC where he attended Southern Evangelical Seminary. Toby graduated cum laude in 2009, earning an M.Div. with an emphasis in Classical Apologetics.

Toby and his wife, Kristina, married in December of 1995 and have two children: Kaleb and Madisyn.

9 780692 220801